LOVE PASSAGES

A Poetic Love Series

LOVE PASSAGES

A Poetic Love Series

Book 1

HOT PINK
NAIL POLISH
AND A BROKEN
Heart

Ms. Tabu

First Edition by Mic2Soul Publishing, February 2020

Book cover design: LLPix Designs

Author Photograph: Robert Cooper

ISBN-13: 978-0-9861728-3-0 (Paperback Edition)

Printed in the United States of America

2 0 1 7 9 0 2 0 0 7

This book is printed on acid-free paper.

For every girl or woman whose ever had her heart broken and mysteriously found the courage to jump back into the sea of love, knowing that the ocean floor might again disappear beneath her feet as the waves come crashing in without remorse.

CONTENTS

"Perhaps someday I'll crawl back home, beaten, defeated. But not as long as I can make stories out of my heartbreak, beauty out of sorrow."

- Sylvia Plath, *The Unabridged Journals of Sylvia Plath*

"But you can't forgive without loving. And I don't mean sentimentality. I don't mean mush. I mean having enough courage to stand up and say, 'I forgive. I'm finished with it.'"

- Maya Angelou

Them Aren't Ready Men

Everybody knows a brother like this.
Most women, have in their lifetime
experienced his version of a relationship,
only finding it to be, quite relation-less
Aside from the bedspread, where
fabricated bliss was followed by
fornicating lips, that led to
confusion caused by a chemical fix
without any legitimate reason
why she should be involved with him
But her emotions, kept her seeking
more of a commitment
from a man, who clearly... wasn't ready
despite his always willing body
Hypnotized by compulsively lusting eyes
He was not cut out to be,
the type of guy she truly wanted in her life
Every time she asked him why
they couldn't move to the next level,
he said he wasn't ready yet to settle
But get this...
the invitation to his house
was always open,
so she stayed determined
but the invitation to his heart, never came
Heartbroken over this brother
using her up like loose change,
always there when he needs it
Not recognizing the horse
had been dead since the first time
she let him have his mission completed
But try to tell her, there was never something more

She'll insist, he really loves her
but just is immature
If she'd only self-reflect for a minute,
she would see that it's a lack of self-respect
keeping her with him
and that every grown woman knows
when to leave it alone
Even if she momentarily trips,
she can pick up and go
rather than sit home, crying by the phone
how he hasn't called her all day
when she should be telling him
not to call her at all
but she's too busy dwelling,
on the memories and the thoughts
Does this woman sound strangely familiar,
like a woman you once were, or are right now?
For those of you who have yet to learn
Let me tell you, them aren't ready men
know how to make sure you are
getting ready for them to get down
All your feelings will be exploited,
soon as the lights out
because these men, aren't interested
in making you a wife now
or even later
Every woman has been there, done that
So do yourself a favor, wait for the one that
God has chosen
Don't waste prayers on a brother who
keeps you going,
in circles

Sacrificing
your own beliefs
just to be his next freak
Next time a brother tells you,
he isn't ready…
Listen!
And tuck your heart
back in your sleeve,
unless you are ready
to get hurt all over again.

Fourth of July Blues

"Do you want to go?" No.
I'd rather stay home with my Keyshia Cole
than put on a show just to please your folks
You asked me three times if I want to go
but never seemed to decide if you want me so...
I'll lie low, give you space, let the tears flow

I think your pride won't let you admit
that I don't deserve to cry over what you did
It's a simple fix, but men would rather keep it broken
They always wait for us to do it for them

I think you know you've made things worse
You just wanted the control back,
Now, what's it worth?
You know I'm hurt and this isn't the first
"I love you," we still blurt,
but those are only words

When actions don't match,
when the passion's lacking and you won't take back
words you spoke when you told me to leave
after all those times, I could have righteously

You know I didn't do anything
although you'll pretend
that's what you think
just to make it sting

Out of spite you shout
"Shoe's on the left foot now!"

So I know this is about,
the times you've been caught out

And it's about, how you'd rather call it quits
before I could get too fed up with your "ish"
to stick around

Why can't you just, spin me around?
Kiss my body down
to that place that's only yours

Do you not want to taste
my sweetness anymore?
Do you not miss those days,
lovemaking when the rain poured?

Even when we were poor,
we were happier before
Now you won't even hold the door
for your lady no more

Maybe next Fourth of July,
we'll get it right
But apparently tonight,
I'm still not enough woman to
introduce as your future wife

So I'd rather stay home
with my, Keyshia Cole,
than put on a show just to please your folks.

Yesterday Was It

Yesterday was it.
Oh, I'm so fed up with this,
his, mine, our, garbage

I slept alone on the floor
Said I don't need this boy of a man, anymore
Yes sister, I swore

But then I began page-digging
through our scrapbook
You've got me tripping,
am I that hooked?

"I've gotta go, gotta leave,"
on some straight up Vivian Green

In my mind I was packing things,
but I opened my eyes
and I'm right back in the ring,
love-boxing
gasping for a breath of oxygen

Brain processing,
mental cyclone
When I vent,
there's no telling
when I'll let go

Got to get through but I'm so lost
I used to know how
to align your heart

Used to see eye-to-eye
Now it's just neck-to-neck
You used deem me with pride,
as queen of our nest

Now your tongue
only consists of bitterness
with occasional fragments of
our withered bliss
It only lasts moments,
until the next feud
This love has become a project
and Elmer's glue just won't do

Yet in the midst of all this,
we still manage to find some happiness
when yesterday's heartache
becomes today's bed break
and I suppose there are days
when we are at our best pace
when everything's moving smoothly
as it did before
But then foolishly,
we're arguing some more

The thing is,
we really have nothing to be mad about
Even our friends look envious,
when what they have doesn't amount
but we just keep on sabotaging
How long will getting our freak on

bandage the forgotten issue,
that we don't really have one to begin with?
It's all in our creation, and we've lost it

We're so deep, got our roots wrapped with weeds
Wish I could hold your heart captive for just one week
Get you back to feeling what I'm feeling,
what we're sealing beneath

We're just scared baby, that's all this is
That's why yes turned to maybe
and we've skipped forgiveness
when the bed breaking comes so naturally
but it's time for communicating, no passively
half-ass sweet gestures

Baby, this thing can be immaculately better
if in yesterday's heartache, we find today's treasure
because even a sunken ship has in it a worthy memoir.

I'm Jealous

You want the truth?
She could be that bombshell, or that nasty heifer
Gorgeous as a prom belle, or ugly with skin leathered
She could be worse, or better-looking than I
A low-cut shirt, or dressed like one of the guys
I'm jealous… because I've wounded pride
I've never felt this, because I doubted those other guys
But you, I kept on that almighty pedestal
only to find that you're human and might be capable
The context of my findings was enough for shit to hit the fan
It couldn't have been worse timing...
I'd just left Connecticut for Michigan
and I know that you say you'd die before slipping up
that you were joking in play; she backs your alibi...
"It's true he was kidding, loosen up!"
But… it's been so hard these past four months
to just forget about what devastated my trust
The vindictive, jealous type was never my personality
but this vicious green fight is one I now must beat
and it wouldn't matter to me if she had corns on her feet,
or if she resembled a superstar
that makes men weak in the knees
I don't want no other girl calling you, just to chat
I know I can't always be guarding you,
from other broads trying to tap
But these nightmares been driving me up the wall
Like you were right there cheating on me !
Then I wake up and there you are
But they seem so real, based off my "delusional" thoughts
and the emotions that I feel,
based off of the conversations that I caught
Maybe we should take a walk, maybe we should talk

It's apparent that ever since,
I darn near stalked you like a hawk…
emails, voicemails, your story I never bought
But when you've witnessed what I did,
you see how someone can hurt someone so
no matter how many years they are down the road
so how do I know that it really was all a joke?
Unfulfilled sex banter
between two friends carried too far
Claimed you never knew then,
you were doing something that would scar
Something very wrong any which way the dice gets rolled
So I'm jealous but well taught - we reap just what we sew
And frankly darling, none of this was my doing
You took your bargain, it's your own words you're chewing
You know it as well as I, I've never been the jealous type
There's no jealous woman without an apple picked quite ripe
Never should have took that bite,
should have left temptation alone
Sometimes I think…
I never should have took that flight,
should have left for New York on my own
but every time I look into your eyes, I suddenly feel at home
Completely aside from this jealous hype, deep down I do hope
your eyes are all for me and you own up to your mistake
but I won't let you back until I eliminate,
these green fogged goggles, clouding my view
Yes, beast or supermodel…
it would be in this same hue.

Some Days

Some days I wake up, "Damn, I need makeup!"
Ravage through wage stubs
Last night's sex on my taste buds
Somewhere in this pocketbook
is the lip-gloss that's only promise is good looks
Still, I'm hooked that this Maybelline will disguise…
circles of muzzled cries beneath my eyes
muzzled by last night's bedtime lullaby
eyelids silver lined, like the moon in its prime
Sometimes I feel my life's more like,
a promissory note with no one to cosign
A loan long resigned
like I've borrowed these rhymes
from some genius's mind
How can these be mine?
This cleavage, these thighs
can't belong to a woman shunned of her own shine
Still, I'd spend my last dime in the cosmetic line
if it means he still finds I'm the sexiest woman alive

Some nights, in between the space of his breath
while he dreams I lay, and pray to Jesus
with half confessed regrets
Blessings we take for granted
when forever has us fooled
If my affection seems outlandish,
it's because I love him, yes I do
He's the only man on this planet,
to whom I could be true
but sometimes black seeds get planted,
and we say, do things
we said we'd never do

We argue like enemies
and make love like newlyweds
When accompanied we pretend to be,
the epitome of love at its best
and sometimes we are just that, no strings attached
But there are times when our pasts seem to get the last laugh
weakening our senses, our "demons" want us tempted
Yes, some days I'm guilty of wanting to end it

But today when I wake up,
I won't need makeup to make up
No need to portray that I'm okay
with that brush
Just wipe away that eye mud,
thanking Jesus I'm alive 'cause
last night I thought I'd die of
under-fried love
Yes, it poisoned us just enough
for me to pray to Jesus, in my own skin...
no blush
I prayed that he would cease us,
of our own sin and distrust
It's time to pick up the pieces,
instead of hiding beneath this makeup
Circles of muzzled cries, now become smile lines
Silver lined eyes, now become his
stripped windows to my love un-denied
No longer will I hide my feelings by the bedside
No longer will I be concealing love in debt by,
maximized lashes
No longer will every diary passage
be dampened by "Very Black" tears

No more actress chanting that she has no fear
because baby, we're both scared of
where this all could lead
But Jesus is taking care of us
If we believe, he'll set us free
I'm not religiously inclined,
but I see vividly
there is something so divine
that there could be a you and I
So today I don't need makeup,
just faith and peace of mind
This time when we make up,
it won't be with Maybelline.

Heaven Again

How did we get so high
after being so low?
How did we touch the sky,
when yesterday it was
the same old bull?

Cards on the table,
is it luck of the draw?
Is it because I prayed to the Lord
for our love to restore,
for real this time? Is it really real?
In my mind I hear heaven's chimes

Rose-colored glasses tilted...
I still see two lovers who really feel it
Looking from the outside in,
we're in heaven, heaven again

Will it last? Baby, will it pass?
Is this all an act, all to get it back -
for the moment?

Do you really want it?
Please tell me a promise,
never to be broken
Will you be honest,
no sugarcoating?

Will you stay open,
guard down when I'm around?
Will you break my heart again,
while I'm floating on the clouds?

So scared to get this high
After being so low
So scared to touch the sky
and fall hard when I know…

Every time heaven comes again,
it always goes.

First Weekend Vibe

Remember that first weekend at your house
when thirst was deepened before our second doubts?
I kept the plane ticket, in our scrapbook
but it isn't the same is it? I want it back for good
I still think about that last look...
when you didn't want me to leave
before empathy, became greed
Yes, we were happy.
A month passed before you took the bus back
to get my stuff and drive me ten hours plus to the new pad
This inconsistency has me feeling quite differently
What happened to sweet kisses
sealed by summertime picnics?
Are we blinded by secrets,
revealing each other's business?
Have pulled cards, resulted in skulled hearts?
Privacy battered by the honesty factor
I just want to see laughter, breathe matter
the things that last
Now that Cupid's unmasked,
can we work with what we have?
Or was it just infatuation anchored by facades?
I see your interest fading as it evaporates
I stand alone and empty-handed screaming, "Damn it!"
You're on your darn throne, taking for granted
No! I'm not the only woman on this planet!
But I'm the only one who's been down for you like this
Controlled the grounds when we drowned in the mix!
How could you be so careless with a heart of gold?
I feel more like a parrot, this is getting old
Is the issue nagging wives,
emotionally crippled husbands, or both?

Maybe I'm just pissed off,
or just tired of this lip-gloss
glamorizing my upside down pout
Tonight I need Jesus,
but I don't know his whereabouts
On my knees I beg,
"Please, help us find
a way to get back
that first weekend vibe!"
As I fantasize in my mind…
he comes in
and kisses these tears
from my eyes
But then I realize,
he's not coming in to hold me this time
Not tonight, he'd rather sleep on the couch
But in one week we'll be, mouth-to-mouth
like none of this ever happened
and suddenly our forever
will be back intact when
we finally realize…
we're both still chasing after
that first weekend vibe.

So this is Lovesick?

A bad case of dry socket...
crying for days, eyes like the projects
bloody and red, strife drips on the corners
puddle around the gutter where my body lay
The hustle of two lovers, robbed me of my fate
I pray...
upon autistic stars that fidget more than talk
Their shine flickers on the ridges of my heart
on, *off*, **on**... *off*
Why do fallen angels always pay the cost
for devious intentions of demonic convention?
Swear the Devil's at a meeting, black suitcase and all
discussing how he can, evacuate my heart
I don't think this here is a false alarm
This time it's clear, by the "anti-God" I've been conned
What do they want?
You can have it all!
Just don't take my,
don't break my,
don't chase my baby off
They replaced my deck of cards
with a full house of jokers
Love turned hatred, lost by cause
plowed down by bulldozers
Left me with a broken piece of white picket
just to torture me when I'm weak
by delusion you'll come with it
Pay a visit to my soul,
see it's different from what your ego has sewn
Through your veins it's all cold where empathy once flowed
You resent me because you don't know...
my sincerities diluted by your fear that we are useless together

18

My left foot forced into a shoe that doesn't fit, under pressure
I pull the laces loose; you tie them even tighter
Put a patent on the blues, give me the rights and light the fire
Burn me to ashes, you know I can't live like this
Victim to black magic of the spirits granted wish
Candles lit in hell, it's all a scandal and it's too late to tell
if time will rebel, feel what I felt when I fell vulnerably
You wish me well,
as if you can't bite the bullet free from my chest
Why must he testify for a sin I didn't,
I would never commit?
Why??? No one in my defense,
just shut my lids and call me blessed
So this is lovesick? *No, this is death.*

Sprout

It was so easy for us to talk about…
buying a house, making wedding vows
future children, symbolic tats on our chests
symbolic of all that love we confessed

We thought we had figured out this thing,
loosely delivered vowels as though our hearts were in sync
It's kind of like these rappers, flossing publicly
Believe half of what you hear and none of what you see

We rocked our love like badges on sleeves
Fronting for the masses like we were the epitome
Hands clasped, putting our mark on the map,
strutting through the park, kissing as they walked past

Lonely hearts clocking us on the watch for a clone
not necessarily wanting us, just want their own
They didn't know, that's what's so beautiful…
we were milestones away
from the roles we've portrayed

We created our foundation off of aspirations
talking about our future babies names and
we didn't see it all falling down
I didn't see these crying walls,
all I saw was wedding gowns
Which tiara, which lockets,
which rings we wanted

There's a fine line between
the yearned and, the earned for

I have learned that our being so sure
was our biggest flaw

Our love became more like playing detective,
so much explaining left our nest restless
I couldn't eat right, sleep right
See right, left, or behind me
let alone in front of my face
Too darn busy looking for an escape…

   Each other's

   phones

   emails

   laptops

   we confiscated

unprepared for that mop that bucket
How are we going to clean up that?

At first we adjusted…
figured we'd accept the questionable
but then we're doing it again,
like John Legend here we go

We've tried fresh slates
We've tried to forget and we've tried to erase
because every time we tried to communicate
it just led to the "you's", the "buts"
back to past stuff that grew new buds

I reminisced when we said,
this would never be us…
and then it was
A sudden change in effect
Our human wasn't good enough
for our facades to accept
until we got the first glimpse
of what it'd be to be without
A chance for unconditional love
to finally sprout.

Hot Pink Nail Polish *and a Broken Heart*

I always try to look extra pretty
when I'm feeling ugly, as I do
Mirror, mirror, show me a cue
Have I found the perfect hue?

Hot pink nail polish to
drown my sorrow
Anything to demolish you
yet somehow you follow

so I dipped my mascara brush,
spinning it around and around
Hoping to perish us
as I'm slipping down,
to ground
zero

My eyes swell to match the color
of my Sally Hansen pedicure
My nails become the wishing well
where mascara drops now hover

I wish... *I wish...*
I wish my lips didn't live in the
remembrance of his kiss
how he used to smudge my lipstick...
so I stopped wearing it

And the mornings where we ate pancakes,
he had that sort of stare upon his face...
the kind to make me ask "What?"
just for the respond back of, "Your natural beauty."

He liked me best in my essence
whether that meant I looked perfect
or blemished
so I was sure to third layer
that cake today
as I remember your preference
was my eyes blue or gray
undisguised, you'd rather watch them change
with my mood as they...

sparkled in the sun,
that crept through broken blinds
I thought I saw them sparkle once,
as I reflect to potent times
but that was just the shimmer on my lids
as I rubbed our picture against my fingertips
and they twitched

I can't live
like this
trying to paint over your face
in my reflection
You always find a way to taint clovers
when they appear present

Still, I keep coming
for seconds,
thirds,
fourths
Just keep on letting you
hurt me some more
with the illusion

that my maximized lashes will
blink you away,
away,
AWAY!

Why are you still here?
Aren't I miserable enough, for one
day, week, month, year?

I bought this hot pink nail polish
to drown my sorrow
Anything to demolish you
yet somehow you follow

By midnight I poured out the whole bottle
It went nice beside my smashed eye shadow
and squished lipstick, in my palm
What use is this? You are gone…

hot pink nail polish, *and a broken heart.*

Leaky Faucets

Moist Lips like leaky faucets
Lusts drip echoed through
heart valves like hallways
A sound that kept me up nights
yet simultaneously pacified
this noise in my mind
or rather relevance and sense
deemed annoyance
Rather pretend these moments
were potion than poison
Laziness or rather sessions of late lazy sex
made it quite complicated to leave the bed
"Turn it off. Make it stop."
Brief throbs of need opposed to want
caused a mental glitch
stimulating wrists to twitch
But I lay, inconsiderate of door knobs
and legs to walk toward the light
Make a choice that could bring
peace to the cries my soul silently weeps
as insomnia leached onto my energies like blood
and delusional thoughts of love kept me plugged
Listening to the repetitiveness of each drop
between silhouettes, that won't stop
Louder and louder with each minute
I've grown an obsession
with repressing sleep for this tension
released by compulsion
to toss and turn between sheets
where a fiend sells affection
to ease his erection
Happily accustomed to his company

A high that seemingly comforts me
with torture like summer heat

    Insides **leak**

    like sinks

    as **he**

    sinks **inside** me

Naturally in-sync is our symmetry
and chemistry designed to chemically
sentence me like imported porcelain
to this, his, mahogany attachment
Could it be the physical satisfaction?
or something much deeper that plagues
me with this habit turned passion
gone out of control
I can fix it but… I won't
As much of a disturbance it is, I know
that without him, I'd feel alone.

The Feelings that I've Felt

Nobody could ever tell me,
I shouldn't feel the feelings that I've felt
I could stay mad at me for loving you
and mad at you not loving me...
but how would that have helped myself?
See, somehow I got lost in that sea
when the ship began to sink
like the captain going down with it, too deep to see
all the treasures lost when time lost me
Somewhere in between those hands,
there's a woman wanting to be free
All she needs is someone to believe
she'll make it up in time to breathe
There's so much more to reach for
at the surface than beneath
I'm so ashamed within
that I've forgotten my will to live for me
They think I'm crazy for drowning when I can swim
Need the dolphins like angels at this moment
Shark fins circling my spirit
I would scream if I thought someone would hear it
There comes a time when only you can save yourself
I remember when you told me,
I shouldn't feel the feelings that I've felt
I was so mad at me for loving you
and so mad at you not loving me
that I couldn't help myself
With all energy draining from my body,
how could I be the kind of woman you wanted me to be?
Motivated while in pain? Baby I'm sorry,
for the day I became too human
to fulfill once positive thoughts of me

But did you know a real woman,
never gets here on her own?
In a sea so cold,
even seaweed would have no home
Don't you see you've made an iceberg of my soul?
For a while this was the only thing keeping me afloat
yet love has a funny way of breaking through
I couldn't go on hating the me in you
Sometimes sinking all the way to the bottom
is what it takes to reach the top
No matter what they say,
the ability to love always comes from God
Feelings uncontrollable left my heart vulnerable
enough to stop beating the rhythm of nature
Sometimes ultimate freedom means
letting the waves have their way with you
for long enough to engulf your pleading heart and show you
that you are only as lost as you believe you are
Even the wrong direction will lead you to the shore
Found myself in a place where I'm not mad at you anymore
because somewhere in all this loving you,
I've also found I love me more than I ever did before
you told me I shouldn't feel the feelings that I've felt
while your heart was somewhere else
until the moment you saw me with someone else
Suddenly you were mad at you for loving me
and mad at me not loving you,
but I still do.

Why We Can't Be Just Friends

Well first of all, that best friend spot is already taken
so I really don't need the lame excuses to leave me vacant
Time wasting, we could be lip tracing, love making
Hip gripping, finger licking, sticky lava dripping
hot like a million suns on your volcanic eruption
When they say absence makes the heart grow fonder,
they didn't mention too much absence makes it grow sour
So while you're thinking this could
make our bond grow stronger
I'm here deprived of what I know
I felt when we were lovers
and I think it's completely senseless
for us to hold out any longer
Senseless like the letter that sentenced
my ripe heart for picking
back into the soil where I can't fall victim
Longing to feel your roots again, ravaging my leaves
spreading openly, extracting potently
You are the master of my domain, between the sheets
where I queen the shaft of your organs like
the first taste of hot rain you've had in weeks
I am the harvester of your seeds
The muse to push you harder, inside of me
The softer squeeze that every real man needs
The curvaceous hips around your masculine body
The queen honeybee of your nest,
inside of me I produce it and store it
awaiting you to bring me more sweet nectar
for the honeycombs of my soul
I am the exotic flower of your jungle
The ice in your neck when you drip cold sweat
Do you understand, why we can't be just friends yet?

When we, touch again,
baby, when we touch again
everything will come back again
Emotions running wild, like my long locks
when they cover your face as I'm smithin' on top
Hard like metal baby, my lips florescent with blood
Ready to crown royal every inch
of your every molecule in existence
Ready to fall in love again the way we first did
This is why, we can't be just friends
We've already crossed those lines
We've already rocked and rolled many nights
You've rubbed all the strings of my silhouette
with your fingers, no pick
You've given me the taste of what it is to
do it with and without that "golden fix"
You've made me fantasize about someday
having your, *oh I can't say it*
Baby, I can't say it,
I can't scare you anymore
Baby, this is all your fault,
so why are you punishing me for?
I thought you wanted a real woman
not these broads playing games
like I had any need to compete
Why would a queen be worried
about the average bee?
Go ahead, honey, try out her wings
I guarantee they won't expand
in the way you need
You're the perfect fit, just for me
Tightly wrap me around your piece

Press your feet against my feet
Porcelain and Mahogany, art in motion
Hot orange toe nail polish
has this canvas voting to be chosen
in this romantic auction
Let them do the talking,
baby, I'll do the walking
The highest bidder has already bargained
You know the pocket of their heart
isn't stacking enough for the price
The price of love comes at no material cost
So like I said those other girls
are too broke to know God
I know the God in you
Baby, it's too late to just be friends with you
Baby, it's okay to just be true to what you feel
when it's real you know the deal
Don't "okie doke" me with this nonsense your friends told
Might as well be brainless if your brain is like mold
to anybody who wants to press on your mind
See, I thought that you were mine
I thought the connection was enough to fly high
so why are you cutting on our wings
when we had something royal like fresh springs
never ending, always wet
I have found my wings of forgiveness,
but you've got to earn the redemption
You've got to do work to make the pleasure squirt
Make it all better baby, take away the hurt
I just need your heart, the rest can come later
I know that you want to give me the world
before you ever make me your girl

but I'd rather be your girl through the hustle
so that I can appreciate the history of our struggle
Baby, don't you see these other men
trying to step in your sweet puddle?
Meanwhile, I'm practicing abstinence
because I'm waiting for you to complete my puzzle
This is why, we can't be just friends, no we can't
We already took the chance
So why are you wimping out of
this once in a lifetime dance
that will move you in
every way you want to move?
Don't you remember moaning
how you love the way I do?
You love the way I move
Yin-to-Yang, you know it's true
We can't be just friends when I want you,
how you want me
I know you will come back to free me from this shore
where I sit lonely wondering
if you're somewhere finding you in that deepest blue
as my aura is reflecting that hue
Keep on swimming, do what you've got to do
The pearl of my conch will be here safe for you
to gently pry in due time
This **is** why **we**…
you and **I**
can't **just** be…
just friends.

I Tried

I tried to find the perfect words but I couldn't
All I could find was my heart bleeding on your screen
like a white T-shirt
How can a man walk around denying the truth,
that he took from me everything I thought I knew?
It feels like the stains of my new life on you
are all that remains of everything I was about to do
I tried to tell you not to do it, I'm a good woman!
Please don't pull the trigger baby, please...
you knew you shouldn't!
But it was so easy to be trigger-happy
and jump the gun
What better way to forget me than to hit and run...
pretending it wasn't what it was
All the things you said, all the things we felt
You let them get up in your head, convince your mind
of what your heart doesn't tell
but you signed the agreement, anyway
like a conman offered the right price for the job
I guess it sounded good enough to break my heart
What about the letter, what about my words?
Was the inkwell of my soul not enough worth
to show you what a real woman deserves?
How can you go to sleep while my spirit's crying?
Aren't you haunted by the memories?
Don't you remember me?
I was just there last week,
days one through three
Making love to me, looking in my eyes so passionately
Now, I didn't know it was all a scam
All I knew was what I felt, and I felt you were that man
Now, what happened to your part in the deal?

You're not ready for a woman who can make you feel
Do I remind you too much of a dream you once had?
Now that it became a reality, you're so scared of the past
Thought I told you that I wasn't her
Thought I said I'd never leave a man this good
I don't want to hear it, just stop this pollution
All of this is nothing but lousy excuses
I can't take it anymore, leave me alone!
No, don't leave me, hold me close
Who's going to kiss me now that you won't?
I don't want the other guys who want to
I won't let you go
I don't want to give my body to another man
Why is that so hard to understand?
Forget the time limitations of "when"
a woman "should" feel this kind of way
What happened to listening to our hearts
and the connections we have made?
Don't treat me the same, this is much different!
You and me were already intimate
Don't pretend this wasn't exclusive
when you told me that you told them that it was
I heard you tell your friends I was in the picture
You told me you'd be letting everyone know
it's me and you now so don't change the script sir
This is photographic memory served on a broken platter
Whoever gave you that advice didn't want us to be together
I thought I told you that we have something to be envied
Look at you being attacked by the enemy
Trying to pull that friend card on me
like I'm too dumb to see what it really is
All these other voices up in your mix

Where was your own brain in all of this?
Where was it, please tell me?
How many more signs did you need to know it was me?
Didn't the universe give you enough truth for you to believe?
It's all right there in front of your face
but you still won't pick me up, got me dying of this ache
and you can say it was my presence being all too powerful
as your alibi of feeling inferior for why you took the blow
Was this a crime of passion, did you lose control?
Were you in the right mental state
when you committed loss of hope?
Tell me why our paths have to divide to align?
Why couldn't you do this while looking me in the eyes?
Would everything you think you feel suddenly mean nothing
when you feel everything your heart knows is real
and can't be the one gunning?
Look at this mess you've created
Was it all so perfect that you had to find a way to taint it?
Who will drag my body away
when I'm too strong to say goodbye?
Who will pray for me
when I'm not weak enough for God's light?
Who will answer when I find my spirit at your doorstep?
There is unfinished business here, this isn't over yet!
Let me in baby, please let me in!
Now I know the meaning of begging
How could I be that woman?
But having any man I want isn't what I want
I'll tell you over and over again, I know what's in my heart
Who will make the first call in the midst of pride?
Will you really admit I told you so
when you finally lose your mind enough

to find that muscle bursting through your chest?
I can't be the one to pull the plug on your breath
I'm not her baby; I can't just watch it end
Move on with other men and do it all over again
I've done it all before, I can't do it anymore
When you come back, there's just one chance
so you had better make me yours
This woman's work doesn't come a dime a dozen
I tried to find the perfect words
but all I had was, I love him
I know it's crazy so call me crazy
baby, I have nothing to lose
I knew you were the truth since the first day I met you.

I Tried PT II

I tried many things to get over you
I thought hitting up the salon was right on cue
I thought maybe once I was looking fly
that I could stop loving you
Apparently my hair looks good
and I'm still spilling the blues
Tell me what's a ride or die woman to do?
It's not fair when someone plays you
It's not right when they take for granted
the days you...
were there for them through it all
whether they were rich or poor ,
broke and out of work rolling with no car...
or doing real good, grinding extra hard
Whether they lost a friend who got shot
or they were handling business and
didn't have much time to talk
You still appreciated the time they made
before Satan convinced them, to dig the grave
and bury your love alive in the ground
But didn't you know the roots still thrive,
even now?
Even now...
that I'm fed up with your act
Even now that I wish I wasn't so foolish
in thinking I could win this combat
to think "Soldier of Love" was my theme song
when I'm only a broken dove
when you pull my camouflage seams off
and my only warrior gear, is my skin
Until I remember, in the heat of tears
that God gave me spiritual weapons

but baby, I just don't know which one to choose
I don't know which gun, is the one to shoot
I don't know if the blood of Jesus
is good enough for you
when I've been praying it over our love
since we made it official
yet somehow you manage to get twisted up
in Satan's most basic ritual
to sacrifice love for pride
during divine moments of our life
and I'm trying... I tried... to understand,
why on earth your realization is missing
and most wanted all across the board
God's Kingdom is searching for
the demon who robbed this love
from that heart of yours
I tried to go on my own mission
but the truth is I'm just a woman
not equipped for this expedition
God-given, unless I trust God
and let Him show me different
Still I thought, that maybe
one of my older poems was right after all
Maybe my life is all just...
Hot Pink Nail Polish and a Broken Heart
Maybe I should just buy some more
so I can watch my tears drip down
the cascades of that place where I fall
Stuck behind a waterfall
in between a rock and it's hard
I pray to God and repent
if I've done anything wrong

The only thing I can think of
was giving too much, too soon
I was doing too much seeking
and not enough being found by you
Letting the roles get confused
but I only was reacting to you
I tried to let you be a man, have the lead
but you led us into quicksand
instead of to the sanctuary where we find peace
and then when we were sinking, you blamed me
Climbed up out of it, and said
"Look at she, how she scream, how she be making scenes,"
when you know very well who is responsible
for this misfortune of irony
I used to think we were a team
I thought we were quite sweet
I thought you had promised me
that you'd never do this but I see
that the fruits bearing from the tree
verses the things that you speak
were from a completely different package of seeds
Silly me, but I tried…
I watered them
Nurtured them
Sunned them down
I gave them the nutrients to grow
when I should have let them drown
because this was the trick version of our love
Now I'm standing in a garden of a Satanic overflood
with my only saving grace being my hands
washed by Jesus's blood
and wondering why you would trade

God's unconditional love,
to please an audience that is nothing but star-struck
But would they be there when your hair turns gray?
Would they be there, through sickness and health
when this world leaves you in dismay?
Would they even care if you were okay
if you were no longer on stage?
Suppose the Lord taketh your gift today
and all you have is what you are when you are squeezed
Suppose all of the groupies go away
because dealing with matters of the heart
was not their "cup of tea"
Suppose the industry pulls the plug
on what you deem as being
the epitome of your dreams
just as you're on the cusp of stardom
and now you're sitting there
thinking about me and how
I was the only woman who really
showed you unconditional love
even when you were so heartless
Suppose the Lord was convicting you
to take out the garbage
but instead of listening,
you took out the blessing
based on the illusion
but you bought it, flipped it, sold it
even had nerve to be joyous at the responses of others
as they watched you slip
while I was there trying to rescue ship
And baby, I tried... but I couldn't be "Superwoman",
"Boy, I am only human!"

But I suppose you'd rather the robotic new age
trendy generational ways
of bootlegging love, like bad tapes
Why must people take and taint
instead of have faith
in the actual "release date" and wait?
Stop looking for ways to play and escape
and then push the real thing away
for the same old games
I tried to show him the way
but my precious records need to marinate
in a love that will love me better
than a man who doesn't appreciate
the concept of obtaining favor
from the heaven's above
I tried to make it through this maze
with no one to show me the ropes to swing
through a purple jungle of seclusion
and found myself here naked, cold, and ruined
by a world that will never comprehend
what it is to be loved
by an angel, called woman.

How It Really Felt

What do I do with this gift, with this gift?
I've had it since I was a little girl
when I knew too much, too young
but it never stopped me from the den of lions
No, I had to go there anyway to see for myself
if it was true what they said, about these men
If they would rip me to shreds, leave me for dead
If the vultures would come and pick at my skin
If the maggot infestation would begin
as my last heartbeat faded away with the sunset
If I would be reborn again with a new sun risen
I had to feel the hatred to know what love is
I had to learn the concept of forgive but never forget it
when you meet those lions again and they seem timid
Could they ever really change?
Would it all just be the same?
Does it really matter anyway?
By then, I'll probably be married
with a new woman's smile on my face
with three children who carry my legacy in their veins
By then, I'll probably have a closet full of pocketbooks,
a new pair of stilettos for each day
If only I'm so fortunate enough to live to the next
I'll probably be someone famous
I'll probably be recording albums
with the lost pages of my diary, found
You'll probably see him kiss me
and feel some kind of way now
But it wouldn't matter, anyway
because by then you'll have gone through
a whole slew of woman
who used you and left you like she did back then

when the mind games stole your heart like
the worms of a fisherman
Oh baby, you got hooked
She got you good
I had it bad
I tried everything I could but the story is too sad
to read over and over before bedtime
It gives me nightmares
to think of what you've sacrificed
So I hide behind this pretty makeup on my eyes,
dresses that make me the queen of the night,
and inside I cry just a bit
because I have lost just as you did
but the difference is, I didn't do it
Still, I suffer from your choices
Oh freewill, what have you done to God's sons?
To these men who run from love,
what have you done to my new love?
Couldn't you find someone who deserves this?
Somebody already broke my heart before him
and before the guy before that
I really can't stand here tonight
and watch him dancing with her
like how we did in the past
I know the only time is now
but my emotions are attached
to the memory
Sweet memory, please go
Dear premonitions, why do you haunt me so?
Why did you bring me here?
Why did you tell me he would be here tonight?
I had other plans, and they weren't these

When does this all begin to end?
When can I bend into another shape
so that you can't see the love in my body language?
Why did he come to talk to me outside?
Did he see the sudden rage in my eyes?
Did he hear my girl's husband say how
he was crazy to leave me for that chick
just playing with his mind
and how you were thinking of me
when you walked away with her
but didn't take her hand this time
while I'm on your mind
whispering in between the parts she has infected
I don't blame the woman for your own choices
You are the maker of your own butchered blessings
Count them one by one as I step away!
I can't bear to look at your face
I don't care what you have to say
Sorry isn't good enough
because if you were sorry
you wouldn't have messed it up
when you had a chance to make it right
You'll never know how it really felt
when I saw you put your hands on her lower back
My mental camera snapped until there was no more film
The old me broke like a glass lens
as my body kept dancing with friends
Just keep dancing
until I forget him
Just keep dancing
as the pieces are embedding
in every part of me until I wished I were fleshless

I don't want to feel it...
is it my skin or my spirit?
I don't know any more when it all feels the same
It really felt like I was going insane
It's always this way when the premonitions paint
a perfect picture, just the way it is
Not to mention being an empath really doesn't help
It's hard knowing it all sometimes
It has hurt my heart to know these things
while everyone is blissfully blind
Now, I've left room for human error too many times
then I wished I'd listened to that voice inside
So now when she speaks I will listen
When she tells me that the energy is shifting
I thought she told me that he was different
I thought she said he was the one God sent
and then the universe showed signs of alignment
So who do I trust now?
Sweet intuition, have you deceived me
or was that just my humanity
wanting it to be, needing it to be?
Oh, how it really felt like I had finally conquered sobriety
No longer drunk off of guys who poison me every time
I guess he was just another shot, to my heart and my pride
How it really felt when he lied
when he tried to say he's a good man
when he's just like them based on his actions
Forget his intentions!
Did I mention it really felt like I loved him?
But now I'll pray on my knees to the only man to be trusted
and to the spirit that rose him
Please Jesus, please God...

Bring me a man who knows what he's got
when it's found, not when it's lost
Forget the men I want...
show me the man you've picked
to spend each gifted day of my life with
Could I ever be so fortunate?
Father please, don't leave me in this mix
Please resurrect me from the damage they did
Give me a new heart and mind
so I can be born again as a new woman
who knows how it really feels
to be loved for real.

The Beauty of Being Used

Prostituting your chest
because he concubines my heart
Soliciting my tears on the corners of your lips
I'm going through some changes
and your head feels just like his
Crying to the Lord because I miss it
Wearing your tee-shirt, sleeping in your bed
Thankful that you are giving me this respect
when I'm so weak right now and don't know
what I might do in this state of phantasm
Please don't touch me in that place,
I'm not capable of reaction
Just let the Neo-Soul music play
in the background of my pain
Just pretend you don't hear me cry
but hold me because you do
Don't worry, these tears are pure
as holy water baptizing you
Let them dry on your chest as a souvenir
This is all I've got left, I don't even have fear
and I'm so scared of what I might do
when I feel like there is nothing to lose
All we're doing is holding hands
but I feel like I'm having sex with another man
I'm sorry to use you as a replacement
I'm so sorry, his face I just can't erase it
and I'm not saying you want me to
but it's like I've become the user because I was used
For being a friend and not just a man, I thank you
I'm hoping Lauryn Hill will tell me what to do
as she sings from every division of my heart
like a bunch of wires disconnected and broken off

What kind of man could find the end or the start?
Feel like I'm from a fallen asteroid, here on this earth
I have been alienated by men who butchered my worth
I'm so tired, of being "too much woman"
What a burden it is to be equipped
if there isn't a man in existence
who knows what to do with it
If this was God's gift then,
why am I such a misfit?
Why can't I be loved like any woman
even if I am different?
I'm only human but they treat me
like a cave filled with gold
Prideful of their discovery
but don't know how to behold
so much beauty in the hands of time
So they use me for the only
piece of eternity they can find
Run away like thieves in the night
Why does man run to the dark
if he reached the light?
God please give me some "Peace of Mind"
Send me to some place where I'm not divine
where I can live a normal life
Where I can find
a man who really loves me
for everything I am inside
A man who doesn't feel so inferior
that he leaves me behind
Why is being a queen so taboo on this man's pride?
This is just a woman who holds her temple high
This doesn't mean you needed to roll out a red carpet

All it means is I need to know where your heart is
while I'm lying on his, cherishing this moment
but I'm thinking it's you and he knows it's true
He tells me I'll be all right, but I was all right
when you were here by my side
Why did you look me in my eyes and lie?
Didn't you know my love is like diamonds?
((((It won't die)))
Please tell me why?
Why did he let me believe all those nights?
He knew I'd already experienced
a man who couldn't make up his mind
Used and abused
until I rescued myself from those
emotional, mental, chemically combined, soul ties
Tell me, why did he look me in my eyes
like he wanted to love me
when he had already realized?
Forget the intention,
selfishness was the action
Every day there are good men
who commit the same exact sins
as the bad men they are bashing
How is this any different,
if everything boils down to the same thing?
I don't care now what he may think
He can't judge me for what I'm doing
See, this should be his arms around me
If he's so thankful he found me,
why would he let me go?
If you're a man of your word,
why sell your word to the Devil?

So you say I deserve a man on my level...
What about the level of being real?
What about the connection we feel?
Now you're ripping open
all the wounds you've healed
Tell me what is to be found on this battlefield?
Tell me the beauty of being used
while I'm lying with him, pretending it's you
Hoping the dream-catcher of his spirit
will make this one come true.

I'm Done

Take me for granted but there will be a price
You used to cling to my every follicle like lice
I'm so done with itching from this residue
of all the things I had to do to get rid of you
I really can't bear living another day
with all my energy going down the drain
I know God didn't plan for me to live that way
so I will see you out the door without a trace
I can't erase your face but I can make a change
I can't be replaced but you can call her name
and somewhere in your brain, you're thinking of me
You're what we mean when we say some men are the same
Now, I won't say all men because that's all in vain
I still hold faith that there's a man on the wait
He may not be a virgin but our love he won't taint
I don't care about societal definitions of purity
I want a man whose been through pain
so he can understand me
I don't need a man who grates away
the tribulations that have hurt me
I need a man who knows I've fought many wars
I've won some, I've lost some but I'm stronger than before
I'm so done with being done like a chore
like I am something you just have to do
Any man would be lucky to have a love this true
I'm not waiting around for him to choose between two
I am not the other woman, I've already worn those shoes
They didn't fit right even after a year of breaking in
I know my attitude has a higher concentration
but I didn't get on this here bus alone
so don't be surprised
when those wheels stop rolling

and your stop arrives
That's right, God won't forget about you
Better be prepared for the consequences too
You can run away, "karma" coming for you
You may never pray but His spirit is the truth
It ain't no lie that it won't be apple pie
when that timer rings, a grown man will cry
Nothing was ever sweeter than you and I
but I'm so done with men who live to lie
Why don't you go on and mingle with your kind
I'm done standing in the rain for you
I'm done living in this pain for you
I'm done
sitting on the shower floor
thinking about how
you don't love me no more
I'm done, ain't nothing you can do
I'm never coming back to you
You're so cowardly
in the choices you've made
and the ways you've deceived
It doesn't matter if it wasn't planned
Baby, you're still going to reap
because it sure has been sewn
Don't come looking for me
when the needles start to poke
I hope they dig you deeply
until you're creaming with foam
steaming off of dreams
of you and me that won't go
I hope you wake up in a sweat
I hope it messes with your head

I'm only human but I know God forgives
those who have been victim
to thieves in the night
There is nothing you can do
to fix what you've jeopardized
You will never get to see
another tear drop in my eyes
Not for you baby,
I ain't crying for you
I'm so through baby,
I ain't writing to you
Too many letters sent
that you read with your head
but they never went to your heart
the way I intend
No wonder this love is so dead
I'm done being hexed
You better find a woman
who can love you less
I'm done standing in the rain for you
I'm done living in this pain for you
I'm done
sitting on the shower floor
thinking about how
you don't love me no more
I'm done, ain't nothing you can do
I'm never coming back to you
I ain't got nothing,
just a pocket full of seeds
I don't know where I will plant them
but I know where it won't be
where these vultures pretend to nurture me

distracting me from my harvest
while these insects eat at the leaves of my fruits
I know these wings like the back of my hand
I'm not fooled, these are wings of the enemy
pretending to be my friend
to send me on that road again
No place I haven't been
Lesson learned, always be present
even when the heart yearns
There will always be peasants
hungry for the royal soils of earth
from which the chosen grow
Sometimes they wear the disguise of others
so we must be careful
Know the person for the fruits they bear at soul
Know the worms in the core of the apple
Know the poison before you start to swallow
because when it's done, the digesting can be harsh
Stomaching a broken heart sure can leave some scars
but it's better to be done now than never at all
While the rain may still fall, I ain't standing here no more.

Broken Records

Lag on brothers, lag on
This record here, will keep spinning
I'll spin on and on until there is a man who can feel me
and when he feels me, our records will become one
spinning on the same axis
You and me couldn't make a hit but you still had to have it
Let God be the DJ of when that song will play
Eternity awaits, there is history to make
Every end is the beginning, every beginning is different
Seeking self, seeking growth, seeking love in the above
You thought you heard the same song, but you thought wrong
You see each moment in my life is the remix of the last
This is that Damian Marley and Nas twist,
some brothers can't grasp
This is that spiritual and mental aligning on the same path
This is that physical vessel meets the heart halfway to take act
This is a moment in your life that you can never take back
The only promised time is now,
there is no right chance or right time
I said the time is right now, you can't press rewind
on this album of my life that we can call "Divine"
I guess you'd rather listen to the mainstream
than hear God's vows
I guess you prefer the radio station
to the station of my soul, child
I hope that the same playlist every day,
doesn't kill you on that road
When you realize that this same script is really getting old
And that you gave up something different, a long time ago
Now you want to Dance down the Halls of my Soul
Now you want to Cherine Anderson me with some
"Good Love" and for it to be,

"You and Me against the World", baby
Now you want to sing Gyptian, "She's My Lady" to the Queen
Now that the Beyonce's "Single Ladies" gave you a migraine
So you decided to finally 112 me on some "Let's Get Married"
And you heard through the grapevine someone new trying to
serenade those places you used to marinate
before you had me on this Lil Kim, "Diamonds" escapade
and it took endless nights of Reggae just to ease my heartache
Piece myself together enough to make it to
"The Love Jones Experience"
Thought maybe if I rock the mic tonight,
I'll feel the life inside my chest
Maybe this slow beat will come back to the tempo I need
so that I can get my Ciara "Ride" on this thing called life
get on my feet with that "1, 2 Step" again
and maybe we will meet again
when you stop acting "Like a Boy"
and start acting like real men
Stop listening to your friends and start remembering
the "Unforgettable", how she made you feel "Just like Music"
and the connection manifested into a verbal expression
as you changed the record saying, "Let's Get It On"
I wonder if Jill Scott's "He Loves Me" will suit me then
or if I'll be vibin' with Beyonce's "Irreplaceable",
teaching you your left from your right again
Regardless, this record here will keep spinning
See me spinning, see me shining from a distance
See me become a star and then you dial up my digits
praying that my love "Don't Change" and that
the Musiq Soulchild you knew back then, is still the same
When I used to tag you in my poetry like "Did You Pray?"
But did you know I prayed for you and me every night since ?

Living in the internal "Heartbreak Hotel" like Whitney Houston
You knew my room number but you lost the key
So now Brian McKnight's, "Do I ever Cross Your Mind"
is what you are requesting
Now suddenly you may be young but you are
"Ready for Love"
So you want to know if some brother spitting
that Mobb Deep "Hey Luv" "G" to me
or if Mary J. Blige's "Can't Keep a Good Woman Down"
has managed to prevent me from trading abstinence
for a lustful night on the town
and if the "Grown Woman" feat. Ludacris
is still in me to wear the crown
and if I'll come back at you like the lyrics
"Who you talkin' to baby, I'm a grown woman now"
yeah, "You better tell your Mother
you in love with a grown woman",
because you will need some advising when my "I Tried" poem
now fits you like it once fit me
But maybe Aaliyah's "Try Again" will keep your faith lit
how I kept mine
when Joe had me crying, "Baby Where You At?"
but I knew it was just a matter of time
before pillow hugging
became you gently tugging,
cuffing at the sleeves of my dreams,
pulling me closely, saying you're sorry...
never knew what you had till you lost it
and now the words back then, you're ready to "prove it"
Papoose versing me, regretting how you were hurting me
pulling up the letter I wrote back when
you committed burglary

See, I can't promise where I'll be but I can tell you where I'm at
I'm here pouring out my pain on just another track
changing my status to "Single"
because I thought we were intact,
but now I see the exclusivity was nothing but a trap
And you know these cats, trying to tell me it's a wrap,
"He got a little tap and now he's back on the mack!"
How easy it is to believe it's just that,
when you just made love to me
last week, and every week before that
but you also introduced me
to your best friends and family, explain that…
No, just do like Ludacris and "Move"
because I really don't care to play the friend card with you
We could have been friends too, how hard is that to do?
I never asked you for the world I just asked you to be you
The world wasn't worth losing your heart,
thought you read that poem too
But apparently, "When Realities Become Dreams",
you couldn't handle the idea
of planting your roots deeply next to me
because this would mean that you had to give up the options
to walk on your grown man feet
And apparently, you'd rather roll with chicks that's flocking
than have a woman like me on that Tamia "Poetry"
But you'll still come to my shows, is that so?
well, I guess you'll get to witness me heal a million souls
as my stardom starts to show
and the birth of the new Tabu is finally exposed
I guess there is a possibility for us to be,
but right now we'll never know
and there is no guarantee that there will be a tomorrow

so while we're here I might as well tell you...
that I knew you were the one, long ago
Before I ever met you, I loved you for all you are
but now like The Roots feat. Eryka Badu,
I've got to be a "Shining Star"
and I hope on that day when you finally wish upon
that I can be the woman to make your wish come true
but for now, I think I need a "Window Seat"
until you can learn to love, the beautifully different me
as by then I'll have evolved into a remixed remix
of the woman I am now
but I can tell you my heart will always be,
where it was the day we found.

It's Simple

Break it off
Rock with it
It's really not
that complicated
Love it
Leave it
Lust it
Defeat it
Swallow it
Spit it out
Want it
Don't need it
Lied
Cheated
Side pie?
Believe it
Don't?
He won't
change
for
you
Changed
for
him
He left you
Sink
Swim
Choose
It's simple.

The Candle

When the eyes of two meet
on connecting levels of humanity
A flickering flame is born;
a chance for destiny arrives
beneath the shadows of love
Glimmering at full strength,
a virgin to the death of fate
Passionate heat forms between two lovers
All desires are at once content
Together holding onto heaven's candle
Cherishing each other with fascination
The cure sounds of angels and tastes like forever,
It is a truly delicious state of mind
Feelings as close to perfection as possible
for one delusional moment in time
Slowly eternity becomes poisoned
when one lover appears disloyal
and the other lover turns insecure
Volcanic tears erupt throughout,
burning through sweetened memories
It was a spark once so lively,
once so mutually of passion
melting to its final flicker;
coating each soul with a layer of the past
Both must come to forgiveness with themselves
For it is of no use looking backwards
The future impatiently awaits
and the parted lovers must now heal
Building upon their scars, a castle of faith
while waiting for that single flame conceived by two souls
A flame to live once before death, and forever after life.

You Shouldn't Have

You shouldn't have kissed me
but I let you kiss me
and you shouldn't forgive me
when I say don't fall in love with me
because frankly, I'm not sorry
I don't apologize for the harmony
of the harp of our hearts
angelic soul rhythms
played with jazzy parts
Mixing and matching,
puzzle-piecing
Fitting together a passion,
never muzzled or weakened
And you never should have
saw me on those weekends
when we chilled out after
we rocked and jived on Mics
I never should have been
the coffee bean to your brew
You never should have drank it
when the steam tempted you
and we never should have
known the "Irony of the Situation"
I never should have had to
run off to church to save the day when
We almost made it... *love*
We almost tasted... *love*
We were almost naked...
but I left you with a painting of my pain
signed "I'm sorry, love,"
next to your favorite cup of our silent memories
But I wasn't truly sorry because...

I knew you would remember me
and I never should have written
my stars in your night
I never should have lied when
you asked why I was running away
and I told you, I was running from me
as the look upon your face
was too sad to tell you...
I was running from the love I felt

when we felt

when you felt

when you held

when I hold

when we fell

into the perfect mold of a potter who
never regretted the violin of our rose
blooming inside of the roots I tried to let go
but I'm only a petal compared to
the ever flourishing flowers of our soil
I never should have been so gentle
or showed you I cared about us drifting
until the last hour that boiled
within our hourglass just before the last grain
I came back to tell you...
that I never should have tried
to escape the grasp of divine time.

Fantasy Girl

I don't know what you were thinking baby
but I know you weren't thinking about me
I guess I was better off kept as a fantasy
Maybe then you'd still be chasing me
You waited patiently
but then when you got your chance
you went and blew it, so cliché
I liked it better before
when I didn't let you inside of my door
and now you've slammed yours
on my heart of gold
I know my attitude has been getting fiery
But boy, you inspire me to change up
just the way you did
It's too bad I love you, regardless
but I'm still not willing to put up with this garbage
It's too bad I'm too pretty, too smart,
and too goal oriented
to let you go and make me
lie down in this bed you made
out of craziness in your head
You're a mess
You're so stressed
Oh, you poor thing
Funny because you still slept
while I stayed up crying
and I'd rather be your fantasy girl
than be some overlooked pearl
I'd rather send your brain in a swirl
than let you see me as I curl into a fetal position
Begging God to let there be conviction
before you get away with a brutal crime,

running away with this heart of mine
Did you forget I was for real from the beginning?
Did you forget I'm a real life woman?
Did you forget when you held me in your arms?
Did you forget I've already been scarred?
Did you forget, "Somebody Already Broke My Heart"?
Did you forget all the times you called,
saying we should be together?
Now you're gone.
Since the first day we met,
we've been the queen and king card
but I guess you're the joker hidden behind royal cloth
It's like you forgot those cherished moments
It's like one minute, you're asking me for marriage
the next you switch the script
and you're not innocent so be guilty as charged
Change your plea now...
you know you broke my heart
Everyone can see through a lie
Now if you love me, you'd make this thing right
It's been a while now,
since we've been booked for the same show
Could have been so good but I guess we'll never know
From the first moment you were hooked,
fascinated by my poems
But yet you're the same one denying me so...
I'll face the rejection
And did I mention?
I'd rather be the fantasy girl in your head than
the real life woman crying these tears
I shouldn't have ever let things go here
but I let you be the man and lead the way

You know this wasn't only me babe
I didn't bring this upon myself
You had me dreaming in my heart I felt
you might be him but how can time tell
when you twist back the clock?
You can't just go back anytime you want
We were here in this moment and then it all stopped
Now look at your fantasy girl
She exists in this world
She cries when she's hurt
and knows she deserves
a man who knows a real woman's worth
but to you I'm just a blur
You only refocus
whenever you get the urge to make it work
You fell for the curse but refuse to be delivered
The fact is, I was nothing but a fantasy girl
I thought I was real in your world
We'd spent time together in the flesh
You said you'd never disconnect
But it's apparent that I'm no longer anything
but a last text, a last call, a last email
before I give up on it all
and go back to being just your fantasy girl
But soon, there will be a change of season
and you'll want me
as a real life woman in your world
Don't know where I will be then
so good luck searching for the one you can't replace
I'll be on my escapade but you won't escape
the place I changed inside your heart
that makes the love I gave

run through your main veins
and when it runs short, you'll be in so much pain
It can't last forever if it doesn't go two ways
but you must have been going through a phase
and it's too bad that all of your fantasies
could have come true someday
Thought you were the man for me
but I'll just say you were the fantasy
I had about my wedding day
You made me actually think
I would have your last name
So goodbye to your little fantasy game
You're just another man making a big mistake
Too lost in a fantasy,
to see what's right in front of your face.

Plan X, Y, and Z

So there I was,
editing a friend's wedding pictures
on a rainy night...
thinking about us,
tired of writing text message love letters
It just doesn't seem right
I've poured out sacred places of my mind
I've shown you everything a man could desire
but it seems like...
you just won't light the fire to take us higher
and I'm screaming out, "The Devil is a liar!"
Maybe the truth is, I haven't been praying enough
Maybe God is using this moment
to get me to step my Holy praise up
Maybe you just don't love me the way I thought
But then baby, why do you call every chance you get?
If it was all just a game, then why did you wait
all this time since we met?
I know you aren't emotionless,
heard you cry before
but your heart went from completely opening
to you shutting the door
You didn't even warn me about close-shop
At least have the decency to tell me what you want
so I can go ahead, get my bolt and my lock
and we can just pretend for awhile
that you don't think I'm amazing and...
I don't love your smile
That you aren't in denial
That I'm not a runaway bride wannabee,
going through a trial
Thinking I'm about to just up and bounce

But then I'm here on the telephone...
telling you, "Baby, I feel so alone."
I'm praying one day soon,
on some random night...
maybe it will be a full moon
like the one I watched with you from separate coasts
when you called me to share that moment
before you had to go
and maybe there will be stars that sparkle
like the ones in your eyes whenever I'm around
and maybe you and I will whisper music like
crickets in the night like we did that time
when I lifted your eardrums with poetry
Maybe it's just been,
one minute too long since you could hold me
I know a man remembers more of what he sees
and that's hard to do without you next to me
but if you can see past the vision visually
and make an incision into your soul
now envision me binding together spiritually
against the odds of flesh
I know you keep some feelings hidden
in the bottom of your chest
Even though I'm vocal about my thought process
the truth is as scared as I say I am...
you're the one who is most fearful
of loving a real woman
because you know this is "No Ordinary Love"
but we couldn't stop it so it got the best of us
I have a whole book of love poems
and rhythms that behold the special notes to a song God-given
and baby, you sing that song to me whenever we speak

I read between the undertones of your voice
and hear each peak
when your heart reaches out to me and says,
"Baby, hold on tight,
I'm sorry it's a bumpy ride but in due time...
you'll have the man in me who will love you for life
if you can just let me catch up for a while."
Boy, I know we can't rush but you know my style
Can't settle for less than queen position
Minimum wage in love, feels like prison
So can a lady get a raise?
Baby, we're struggling and you know it's you to blame
when you're busy guzzling down these worldly things
But either way I'm going to love the hell out of you
until we're so heavenly
and I know I drive you crazy but you still take it
I'm your baby and we will make it
I've been there when skies were the grayest
and you've been there when I was filled with pain
through several healing stages
So if we refocus and recall,
I think we will notice this is real love after all
Even though
it's hard
Even though
I'm scarred
Even though
I had to pull a few of your cards
to give you a reminder that I've been hurt before
Don't need it no more
I've been having second thoughts
You love me, I love you more

On that notion why are we fighting
when our prayers can, be answered?
Even though I had plan X, Y, and Z
of how exactly I was going to leave,
God pulled me back and said,
"Invest your trust in me
rather than in man,
because eventually my daughter,
you will understand
that the only X, Y, or Z you need
are my hands."

Am I Delusional?

It's not that no one has ever
broken my heart before
It's not that I'm a naive woman,
I'm sharp to the core
But if you've ever known a love
that can age like wine in an unusual extent of time
as though we've been around for lifetimes
Cupid took his blow at the right time
Folded me up like a paper fortuneteller
and played with my mind
I should have never believed this fella
would ever really be mine
You know he's the type, groupies hyped
when he jumps off the Mic
they want to jump on quick like
and when we met I turned my neck
told him I'm not that chick, got my own grind
Had the brother expression so confused like,
"Sister, I didn't intend to disrespect you
but I was breath taken by the way you
did your poetic presentation
and everybody here wants you including me."
My body said I want you too,
but God's ruling judged me queen
so I held onto my crown
even though we ended up going out to town
Bought me some dinner, even chilled at the hotel
and ever since then this became the trend
after every show, so...

Am I delusional?
Is this like a death
at my own funeral?
Have I passed over
from a broken heart?
I thought my love
was good enough
but as my blood turns cold
I plead mercy on my soul
Lord I don't want to go
I'd rather be delusional

Tell me baby, what's the deal?
You know you make me hurt when I want to heal
I thought we were special but apparently not
You took it to that higher level
then told everybody but me, you rolling solo still
and I got shot down in my soul like never before
You dogged me out, made me look like every chick before
but behind the scenes you be telling me you loving me
needing me, even asking me if you can get the ring
if we could just get married already
And ironically, I told you we had to wait
that we had to pray, do this the right way
but that on one future day, I'd love to be your wife
but this thing needs to marinate
So let's just build in the meantime
and when I considered relocating, that was your idea
I decided I could move there in like a year

and just as I was busting moves, ride or die loving you
You switched up on a lady like I was nothing to you
Not enough man to claim me, you want to do what you do
Still you tell me you care, say you want to be there
Say nothing's changed,
you just don't want to display your business on the air
But if that were the case, you wouldn't have made
an open invitation for the people to hate
and vouch for your mistake
Egging you on to keep heading down the wrong way
and you suck it up like a sponge
I guess it was just for fun
but I'm sorry that your circus act lacks tact
and means that I'm the joke of the night,
the reason why they laugh
This whole thing turned wack like a bad contract
But I'm still hoping you can learn and let this be the past
Quit shelving me like I'm the second best
when I'm the one who turned the key in your chest
We haven't even had sex because I'm celibate
and you already messing with my head just to make me sweat

Am I delusional?
Is this like a death
at my own funeral
Have I passed over
from a broken heart
I thought my love
was good enough

But as my blood turns cold
I plead mercy on my soul
Lord I don't want to go
I'd rather be delusional

I guess you're not secure enough in your manhood
To really rock with a woman this good
I guess you suddenly got cold feet
in the middle of talking about marrying me
I guess you forgot about the things you said to me
like the plane ticket that you were sending me
until I told you plans have changed
after I saw you playing games
I asked you about twenty-five questions
and told you to holla back, when
you make up your mind
If you love me,
why won't it show when the rain falls?
Somebody throw the last rose
and say some last words
I think I just took my last breath
when I told him I deserved better
than this empty quest
I'm far too blessed to let you flex
for your so-called friends
and then you don't even learn your lesson
when I preach the hell out of you
I expect a confession but all I get is
you telling me you love me and half-apologizing

But something tells me your thick head is,
still secretly half-denying what you did was
immature and so wrong
 "I know why the caged bird sings" her song
but I swore to myself I'd be free from now on
and the reason it hurts like new love lost
is 'cause this is the first time in a long time
I've opened my heart as a new woman
I was waiting for my husband
but you got up in my thoughts
One minute I'm done with him
and the next answering his calls
so somebody better pull the plug
and watch the flat line come
when I have no more heart
Let my body go numb
Even with blurry vision, all I can see is us
I think even if they declared me dead
that I would live, for love.

Stay or Go

He doesn't know if he wants to stay or go
He lives on philosophies of, "There will always be tomorrow."
He procrastinates on our love like it's the same old job
He clocks in late, and leaves early
He tries to change up the time card like
I don't see the way our fate, looks blurry
Smudged ink where the real thing used to be
But it's hard to know if I should stay or go
'cause he always comes in, even if he comes slow
Evidently, he loves me to his best capacity
But see, his love is like a speck on the map
compared to my heart, the size of a country
and somehow he crossed the border
I don't know who let him in
I tried so hard to block him from coming over
but now he's already gotten citizenship
He's living in, my soul
It feels like he's the rib from which I'm chose
Things just aren't matching up in our worldly roles
and he's so hot and cold
One minute he's gone, the next he wants to propose
One minute he's doing me wrong,
then he wants to come home
and I don't know if I want him to stay or go
I've got it bad like you just don't know
You say you do, but it's hard to explain
why there will be a sequel to the love they call insane
I swear I've tried to escape from these ties
We lie down together but I never let him come inside
so it's not like this is just a chemical lust ride
But it seems like I love him more than
some brothers before who I did, give my body to

With him, what am I going to do?
Somewhere deep down
where it's hardest to expose,
I have faith that he'll come around
if I walk with him on this road
even though it's not perfect, and he changed up on me
I know he knows I've the worth of a queen
and I know he has cold feet
when he's never been in the role of a king
He never had a woman like me
If I climbed from the bottom up then so can he
and if he loves me enough then maybe
he can just show me he wants to try
Maybe if he holds me while I cry
and feels the tears on his lips he will realize
I'm down for the ride but he's got to provide a fix
and tissues can't do it
The truth is everything is useless
The things I do to soothe it
I don't know what I'm doing
One day I want to leave then I feel tugged right back
I'm angry with this destiny 'cause this love is
weighing down my back, dividing up my spine
I pray that God puts our love on track
'cause I'm too tired to drive
For once in my lifetime,
somebody else has to put forth the effort
Somebody has to decide if this love will be forever
Lord, today I'll stay but tomorrow I might go
I want him to go away and then I dream of him
holding me so close, breathing beside me
I need him to find me where he left me

Stop lying and respect me, protect me
don't let his main intentions be to undress me
Remember the things I've told him
about past predicaments
Remember I'm going through
a process of deliverance
Still healing and I don't need this
Remember how good he treated me
when we were friends
before things got deeper and
the things he said
Was he just messing with my head,
or did he really mean it?
I don't know anymore but I know his little secret
as much as he acts like he doesn't need it
he always seems to be phone reaching
even when we pretend we're done with it again
I've told him I was done with him
and I guess I look stupid for talking so much "ish"
when you know the truth is I still want his kiss
I keep praying for God to remove him
if he's not my husband or to move in him
if he is and tell him something
I can't do this alone, all by myself
I need some spiritual, Christ-like help
I need somebody to understand what I've felt
Don't just tell me to leave him
because it might be Satan trying to send him to hell
I want to save him but I have to save myself
I know the Devil wants our men to believe
that Adam and Eve were nothing but a story
I know he wants our men to miss the boats

MS. TABU

stay tempted by these broads who act like hoes
I know he doesn't want us ever to be whole
with the one who is the missing part of our soul
I know that this warfare is spiritual
and if I didn't care, I wouldn't be here with my Bible
seeking revival and survival
a way to win before I decide to go
but if I'm staying then Lord, you've got to let him know
that he's about to lose a good thing
and he needs to quit destroying roots so they can't grow
He's about to miss a new blessing for the same old
and if he wants to make it to heaven
then there's only one way to go
I'm pleading mercy on my baby's soul
I know he's being stupid but I can't lose hope
I know he hurts me but…
I somehow have it in me to still try a little
Maybe it will get better, maybe it won't
but if I just go, then I'd never have known.

Too Much but not Enough

I'm too scared to say I'm scared
I'm too hurt, to say I'm hurt
I miss you too much to say I miss you.
but I love you enough to say I love you
I guess that really says it all
I mean... what else needs to be said?
It's funny how the words that fall
whenever it's raining in my head
never seem to get you wet
I mean like... how is it,

    sleeting

    hailing

    pouring

    flooding

the darkest alleyways
of this unfamiliar place
and still you manage to stay dry?
My feelings undermined... why?
How do you get to the point
of being so unaffected
where you can't hear a human voice
delivering a spiritual message?
How do you get to be the criminal
giving me the jail sentence?
It's like in your mind
you finish each sentence I've said
with a mutated version
of what's actually expressed

It's like you're the echo caving in my head
You're the cold hidden place
where our treasures were left
but I'm no architect
I couldn't tell you when
we created this language
we both used to speak
I can't tell you what these symbols mean
I don't know about this pottery
where hearts were molded and then broken
but I'm too broken to reopen
I'm closing and yet somehow, you again!
Entering like you didn't see the sign
You're saying things that make me think,
maybe I need more time to decide
before I give this all away
I keep unpacking packed boxes every other day
because I'm too alone, to be alone
I'm too beautiful to have no one behold
I'm too soulful to be sold
I'm too hopeful to let go
and you know that you know too much
to pretend that you don't
You can't look in my eyes and pretend that
you're unaware of the history of my life
You can't ignore the soundtrack of my soul
playing music that you hear
even when you say you don't
You can't walk around forever
like you're immortal
You don't need an umbrella
You don't need a coat

You don't need my love
and you don't need to come home
You're only dry on the outside
Look at you, drenched within
Your heart is shivering
but you'd rather catch pneumonia than give in
Too stubborn, to listen
Too hard headed, to be soft
Yet too much time invested
to just give no time at all
So you call to say what? Who knows!
But it's still your voice I love too much, to let it show
If I told you the things I'm feeling,
you'd see too much leeway to get your way
When God says the man should lead us the way,
He means through Him, not through a delusional maze
So tell me am I too lost to be found?
Do I have too much heart to be crowned?
Am I too much a star to come down to earth now?
Too many thoughts to think about...
Tell me where are you now?
You're too far to hold me, not in arms reach
It's too hard to get through this adversity
when you can't see what you've done to me
when emotionally I can speak even if I speak deep
Poetry is poetry, words are words
Even if they are from me, it's not the same
as being next to each other
where telling a lie is too hard
Feelings denied isn't worth the scars
and you realize you love me too much
to keep breaking my heart

but it was much too easy
when we were so far apart
and I'm too smart for my own good
to know that you are secretly
wishing we could make this thing right
for everything you did wrong
but you're too wrapped up
in your own web of lies being self-preyed on
to save yourself before the last candle melts
and I'm all wicked out
but I have too much passion to let us die now
Still got a little flame left
It's not much, but it's enough to see my ink
leaking from the clouds
He's covered too much in me to not see how
he's the only man painted in the whole town
from the palette of a woman who love's too much
but didn't know how to make a man see
that she's tired of loving under his limited warranty
only to be left with too many seeds
and not enough essential needs for these to grow
Not enough sunshine in these poems
Not enough water in your soul
Not enough air for new life to show
We've lost too much of this season
for our harvest to come in full
It's not perfect, but it's doable
but it takes two and I'm here alone
When too much is not enough, it's a dead end road
and now there is nowhere to go.

Broken Bouquet

Boy, you throw me back like a bouquet
Somebody catch me before I run away
A damsel in distress, I can't help it
I'm a candle melting
Call me a criminal, say I'm a felon
Stealing your heart before you can break mine
Many nights I thought I could love you for life
then you change my mind
and I don't want to cast pearls before swine
I thought you were a king
but if you're not, then it's alright
Been independent minded since I was about five
So if you want to be mine then be mine
and if you don't then don't
but if I'm not the only woman you want
to sing you bedtime lullabies
then let the truth ring like church chimes
I don't care if you're hurting in your pride
when you were the one who hurt me inside
in a place beyond the surface of your lies
If I wanted a man who acts a child,
I'd get one who's my age
and put these older brothers out of style
Seriously, I'm tired of you being grown as ever
but yet you act like gentlemen retired
and I'm searching for lost feathers
of angels that stopped guarding hearts of good girls like me
Whatever you say, I'm putting up my guards
I still believe there is somebody out there for me
I'm young but I'm ready, been this way half my life
Don't want to hear me preach because it stabs you like a knife
I'm hitting sensitivities and you're convicted to find a wife

Stop seeking one nights
If you think that my type comes a dime a dozen
then go rock with your dimes and I'll stay single, no fronting
If a man does me wrong, I will dump him
I don't have no mercy, I'm just a human being
So baby, if you hurt me remember... I can leave
I have options all around me but it's not about that
Say you're glad you found me and I don't doubt that
but your intentions are suspended in midair
Did I mention sometimes I wonder if you even care
about the heart of a woman
who has been through worse things?
You shouldn't play with fire
because when my battle wounds sting
I can't make any promise that it won't get ugly
If you love me then just love me
but I won't change my dreams
just so you don't run from me
If you aren't the one for me,
then go kick it with the dummies
become one with my ex-files
They say to kill em' with honey
but I'm just not one to fake a smile
If I feel it, I'm real with that realness so hear this...
if you don't like it then why you been here
the past year with expectations for us to be together?
When I gave it a chance
you took me for granted like the weather
Well, it's about to change... we're headed toward December
I'd rather stay warm but it's about to get cold
when I'm no longer yours and you're all alone
Sorry you forgot to put your woman first like Jaheim wrote

You spoke a lot of words but you fell off the boat
drowning in your own right
and yet my crown is still full of might
Strong enough to say that I love you but I can go
if loving you means giving you the extra mile for the same old
Giving first and getting fifth place
when you'd rather play games
Well boy, enjoy your cake and eat it too all by yourself
I've got better things to do than walk with you to hell
I'm on a path to heaven and can't stop for no man
But believe me when God sends him,
there will be wedding bands
that signify more than a man just wanting my celibacy card
Can't play that hand when it belongs to God
You're so confused
You don't know what you want
I'm a woman of vision with no time for hindering
my God-called position so get with it or get out
Either be monogamous or bounce
You can't call us exclusive and then be ready to pounce
on the next chick with the right features at the wrong time
Brother, if you don't comprehend this…
I'm saying either come deeper or lose me by your side
I may be a keeper but I have standards and a will to abide by
the Holy Spirit's high demands even if they make me cry
when I never really wanted to say goodbye.

Raining Broken Hearts

It's raining from my broken heart tonight
because you're a liar
You're so stupid
You're not even worth the music
but the songs keep falling from my eyes
Nobody seems to understand
why I cry and why I love you
but I hate your way of living life
I hate the things you do
I hate the moment you became untrue
I hate the way you can't tell the truth
I hate your lousy, cowardly excuse
I hate that lack of Jesus in you
I hate your sins and even tried to hate you
But what's a woman like me to do?
I've become a gentle cloud in the softest hues
I try to pop off at the mouth
but then my heart's a fool
Why do I choose you?
If I never knew you, I wouldn't feel this way
I should have continued to run so far away
Now I see the red flags written all over your face
Screw you and your other life
Brother do you like, "Who needs a wife?"
Just watch the years go by…
before you know it, you're fifty-five
with no woman by your side
When family members die
and friends are out of sight,
I hope the groupies still fill the void
every time you press rewind
and all you can think of are my pretty eyes

and all the poetry I'd write
when I told you what I felt inside
Took the risk, but you didn't deserve it
I'm so glad I didn't make love to you
because you like to see a woman hurting
How can you be joyous off my pain?
You know I'm anointed and you won't get away
with the heart that breaks in your hands
You just keep squeezing but I will take a stand
even if it seems I am losing my strength
Trust me, I don't need a heartbeat
to haunt you in spirit
Oh love, you will remember me
I want the days back when
you were a real friend to me
How did those days pass?
Like just yesterday you were
saying how you want to marry me
but how many tomorrows does it take
for a man who borrows time just to be a snake
to be damned by the own bed he made?
But I am not going to be your love slave
So take whatever you want to take
But you can't have my sacred place
You can't change the fact that I'm saved
You can't even look at my face
when you see my eyes filled with rage,
you realize I'm well aware that this was all staged
You and your stupid comedy skits
Did you forget to keep the profession separate?
Has your entire life become a joke?
Well I'll show you a funny bone

when I'm mimicking how dumb you are
when you're finally the one with a broken heart
Shoe on the left foot, soaking wet
from the same puddles that I been stepped
when my tears poured from the sky
and I gave up being yours
because you made me cry
Claim to love me at the same time
Well, your love sucks like lukewarm pie
and I bet you're sobbing
because you can't have mine
I'm waiting for my Holy knight
to rescue me from this rain
It's like a canvas with running paint…
everything is ruined,
it doesn't look the same
Go ahead and throw it away
I'm too drained to care
about the way we used to hang
in a special place
where love could be seen
but now it's damaged and
it will never be the way
it used to be
So get your silly watercolors
away from me
while I await for a palette
that blends beautifully
Because real love is never ugly
so get your fake piece
of garbage out of me
Find somebody

who will treasure your trash
If you really loved me you'd have…
never replaced the gallery of our love
with your wack act
Go ahead, you're up for grabs
This won't be the best I've had
God's got a better man
planned for me than that
A man who will cover me
instead of drown me
in the rain and laugh
and when you see me kissing him…
I can promise that I won't look back.

Avalanche

It's about to be an avalanche baby
You've messed with an ice princess
This is my Mother Nature freedom chant
Soon you will be frozen in our love
Soon you will be suffering,
needing me to warm you up
and rescue you from the overflood
Oh, baby did you think you'd just
provoke me over and over again?
By now you know me
to be outspoken, highly expressive
Yes, my snowstorm within has now manifested
Oh, I hope you're dressed for the weather
I hope you're a soldier of spiritual warfare
If not my love, you're in for a ride
We'll see how you like it when you slip and slide
Every time you try to climb,
you'll find yourself deep inside
the womb of an avalanche
that has no mercy for pride
It doesn't hear your cries
All of your tears become ice
and all you can do is scream for your dear life
"Please save me, I apologize
I know you hate me
for bringing misery into your life
Give me one more chance
I'll love you right this time!"
But baby, I kind of like
watching you try to break the ice
I need to see how serious you are
I need you to breathe the cold air of my heart

It used to be warm but now it's arctic weather
Why did you mess with me?
You should have known better
There's still an ice princess in me
and you sure did test her
Yeah, you pressed her
into the snow with broken wings
and now it's my pleasure
to fly around free
just the way you said
you wanted me to be
while I watch you be
the caged bird that sings
Oh, how the tables turn
with what the seasons bring
I don't think the lesson's learned,
better keep begging until it stings
Have you gone numb yet?
Do you feel the burn in your chest?
Do you feel the avalanche
crashing into your head?
Would you give anything
just to melt this ice princess?
Tell me your plans A through Z
One of them better be
to ask God for the key
to my heart that hasn't enough heat
to melt again for you
You messed with me when I was your best friend
You recklessly stepped into footprints of demonic men
I'm sorry you wanted to be like them
Do you think this is the way to heaven?

Do you think that even hell could
melt this message being delivered so cold
so cold, to your soul?
It's time you stop getting away with
trying to serve both the Devil and the Lord, it's impossible
When this avalanche comes down,
you're going to know who matters most when
your life is on a tightrope covered with icicles
that couldn't care less if you fall or you don't
Somewhere in your chest you remember
the days when I plead the blood of Jesus
on your heart, body, mind
while anyone else would have watched you die
and go to hell as long as they got to be by your side
There was your princess melting for you like ice
For you, I did anything
After all, love takes sacrifice
but it's time for you to have some alone time
when the only thing you can do is survive
and pray that your ice princess
makes it back to you, in due time
This is the avalanche of love,
a spiritual weapon of mine
Boot camping you into a Jesus thug
until your essence is no longer swine
But you can't run and you can't hide
No camouflage, just naked skin
frost bitten, being given new sight
You're about to see things from my side
You'll thank me later when your flesh dies
Consider this a spiritual incubator
that will save your life.

Change the Locks

Heart opened. Heart closed.
Key locked. Keys thrown.
At least I thought...
but you've made copies of your own
when you bootlegged my love
It wasn't ready to be released yet
but you couldn't wait and I wouldn't chase
Still you played tag and said "You're it!"
I found myself running around losing sense
Don't know if I should pray or repent
If I should praise or worship
but I'll take the full package
and board the deliverance ship
I'll sail away on waves of forgiveness
and remember the beautiful words you said
before that one sentence bruised my softest spot
Vulnerable wound I forgot, until I felt it throb and it hurt
like a piece of broken glass in my foot
Turn it over but you can't see the sliver cutting into you
no matter how hard you look
How could something so tiny cause such a mess?
It's becoming quite likely that I may disconnect
Call upon God for the horse and carriage
Runaway bride with no reason to stay for this
This, first last kiss
I'd rather end this and re-begin
one day when there is a new irony to our situation
When listening isn't dangerous
When my feelings know when to go deaf
to the sound of a spiritual love concealed by secular cusps
When I don't have to see your hand against my window
tempting me to put mine up and I can almost touch

but there is something in the way of us
I'm not sure if its protection or love being neglected
As you tuck away diary pages of me into pockets of you,
I hope you find the strength to open up to the truth
I will pray for you, darling, I already do
but this was like a joyous playwright script,
gone melancholy
I suppose this requires more practice
before we take the leads
Maybe we should just dumb down to being "extras"
for this until we can act out this scene so perfectly
Make stage curtains smile as we take our bows
Perhaps I'll see you next time around
in different clothes auditioning our roles
but until then this costume must go
It just doesn't fit when the scripts we read
became too realistic like we were really it
It was safer when we weren't
and now you enter whenever you want
so now I must change the locks.

Real Life Princesses Get Hurt

No, No baby
I don't think you get it
You can't just go
play with a downright
good woman like this
If you throw it then
you better go fetch it
I'm not being dogged around
Tell me the cost a man pays
for trying to rob my crown?
You know I think about
the "What if's" in fast forward
What if I'd slept with you
and then you acted like this coward?
"Made the juice go sour" like Karyn White's song
I guess you thought I'd be your "Superwoman"
and drew some conclusions
like you could do what you want
and string me along
Live another life,
separate from the one that is gone
But you need to realize,
the only life you get is one
and you're living life wrong
According to who?
Why don't we check with God?
None of this adds up next to the Word
we both claim to read
It's not doing any good for me to try and teach
I make it even worse every time I preach
must be the prophet in me, she's a little too deep
I shouldn't wear my heart on my sleeve

but honestly, I held out for a good year
Took the time to build a friendship
make sure you were sincere
and somehow it didn't matter, anyway
I'm still a fool floating on clouds of
"He'll wake up one day."
But by then, you know the way the story plays
The player gives up the game and
the good girl is engaged
then he's on his knees and he begs,
"Baby please, don't marry him
this time I'll stay!"
Claims he's prayed, says he's changed
Says God said we should try again
and I should erase
the way I've been living since
he's been gone
Like I should have an Etch-A-Sketch for a heart
and just shake it up for you babe
Well, you didn't shake it up for me
You had your mind made up
before even praying to God to see
if the Devil was just making you slip into a sleep
so you could easily hurt me without feeling the way
it stings the union made
between two lovers meant to be
What about destiny?
What about missing out on your blessing, see
this will hurt both you and me
This isn't just a one-way-street
Soon you'll come up out of this dream
But by then, I might not want to speak

When the trust goes then how can love be?
So you say you love me enough to set me free
but if you really loved me you'd have communicated to me
You can't just go making huge life decisions
that affects both parties
though on different ends
and act like I don't have a right to be hurt, mad, and sad
I need you bad but I want to leave your a..
Why I had to cuss you out just to get half the truth?
You know the way it sounds
is like you found yourself an excuse
to run from a real love so true
I guess you'd rather be miserable
with a circumstance you already left behind in the past
but now suddenly you find a reason to justify turning back
in the middle of our relationship
and you had nerve to not even be saying it
Just leave it like a blank script
Like a tape that won't play,
it used to be my favorite
If I even had the ability for hatred,
I swear I'd hate you
but ever since my life changes like salvation
my heart is brand new because I prayed specifics
Boy, you need to get with it
Speak to the Lord like He's your right-hand man
Pray in advance and just listen
Don't make a move until He says so
But you will do what you do if you won't let go
of your worldly control and fill your role
I tried to fill mine
If you want to know why you make me cry

This is the first time since my days before Christ,
since my new life that I gave a man a chance
Even though I ran for some time...
I still kept you in the loop
I never lied to you
I told you the reasons why I was scared to
Never gave a lame excuse
I never planned to meet you
through all them shows on my coast
I tried to keep you at a distance
but you became a main part of my circle
Matter fact, you were the centerfold
And you know...
I never kissed a man since the last time I saw you
And you know...
I was waiting for God to call you
And you know...
that I liked you enough not to slip up into lust
And you know...
the man you'll see me with one day
could have been us
I should have kept the poems about us
at the first ones
"Irony of The Situation,"
and "Ain't Rocket Science."
I should have never
let the situation produce all these rough diamonds
with edges to buff
that shine timeless
What's inside them? Love!
Who designed them? The God above
So why we fighting? Because he betrayed us

How can I adjust this new clasp to fit when
the picture has turned back
to being a figment of my imagination
Open the locket, *what's in it?*
A blessing left behind and diminished
A wife who was sent to a man
who trashed himself gift-less
If I'm from his rib cage
then why does it feel more like I'm in a cage
If he is setting me free,
why do I feel like he has imprisoned me?
I'm slowly becoming like Alicia Keys
on Def Jam Poetry, "Prisoner of Words"
but God keeps using me
even though I don't want to speak
Somehow the words find their way to leak
to where the whole world can see
and I must look so crazy, so weak
so... melancholy
But who cares what they think?
This is more than poetry
This is me trying to take back the key
so you can't come in and peek at me
so you can't have the luxury
of witnessing the beauty of a woman
who loved a man unconditionally
even if she makes him think
that she never wants to see him again
Still her ink develops photographs
of everything they could have
Memories snapped
I want to crumple every poem

and throw it in the trash
I have a whole book about our love
through the times we had
and it's sad that it has to end sad
Nobody likes an unhappy ending
but I'm sorry this *Cinderella*
doesn't get her glass slipper returned back
I'm sorry *Sleeping Beauty*
doesn't get to wake up from his kiss
I am sorry real life princesses
go through real life predicaments
So forgive this unhappy ending
and tell the little girls to dream again
even if it doesn't seem worth it
when they see grown princesses cry
It's a shortage of prince's
and an abundance of cowards with
way too much pride
and a lack of gentleman
when the clock strikes
I'm sorry to tell you
that nothing magical happened
this time at midnight
I'm sorry real life princesses
don't always get what we deserve
Men say a lot of words
but like an abandoned church
being sacred doesn't always mean
they will value your worth
At least I'll still be precious in the eyes
of the one who favors those who serve Him first
I'm His princess even when man-made castles burn.

Sweet Girls Go Sour

Now I know the way the story goes
A good tree can't bear bad fruits
and a bad true can't bear good so...
I know the way it looks
when I let this side of me show
But if you listen close,
you'll see that deep within my soul
this bad girl act is all a pose
I'm sweet to death
but I can get mean if you cross step
and even the Bible
speaks on times when we must take defense
refute every tongue is our heritage
and we must sometimes use spiritual weapons
But I'm human and sometimes...
I just want to cuss them out for hurting me
when I was nothing but a good girl
all the way around
from the first day he came to my town
It's over a year later now
I thought I knew him well
But what we know verses what we've felt
aren't always on the same page that tells
the stories of our minds, bodies, souls
and while all three should unite
There are times when they don't
There are moments in life when,
we just need to grow
when one side of us is at a more advanced level
but the other has a long way to go
and when it comes to me and him...
I see that we need much more than feelings

I understand we need to experience life together
and there isn't really any guarantee
that this will be forever unless God wills it so
If I think I'm in control of the leaver
I've been misinformed and need to let go
Make some room for the Lord to do His thing
Sometimes we try too hard
although we think we'll make it better
yet only make it worse
Sometimes we think we're so cleaver...
acting out of spite when we're hurt
I know I've said some things
I know I put him out
but he kept messing with me so,
my last nerve came out
Some may judge me for exposing the real
but the people who love me
know I speak how I feel
I'd rather voice my thoughts
than live my whole life inside of a box
whether it seems personal or not
when I write my poetry
Some people think I should watch the way I talk
but if I were to change up my transparent walk
then I wouldn't be walking with God
and if people want me to only write good things
then they should treat me better
if they don't want to pay the cost
of being a "slave to my rhyme book",
like the song by Nas
But you know, at the end of the day
I'm softer with every hour

As the night goes on and loneliness prolongs...
the slow jams come on and I'm wishing
I had my man to take me in his arms
Some people say I have too much heart
but I say people don't have enough
Some people only call when their life is hard
but don't care about the ways you suffer
When sweet girls go sour,
let me tell you the deal!
Somebody must be
trampling on our pearls
to devour all the sweetness we feel
It doesn't just happen overnight
Good girls don't just go bad
with no reason in sight
There are things you don't see behind the scenes
The way people have hurt me in my life, repeatedly
They don't know the battles you've fought
They don't know that sweet as you are, you are strong
Sweet girls only go sour
when somebody does them wrong
So tell me baby, what do you want?
Because I can be so sweet,
but I can be many things
depending on the destiny bought
If taking me for granted was worth the expense
then you best believe the damage
will burst through a vent
What goes in must come out
So when the sweet girls go sour
ask them whose putting misery in them now?
See, when the sweet girls go sour ,

people stare in such shock
She was so sweet but now she's hard as a rock
But when the sour girls act sweet just to deceive,
it seems nobody questions their identity
However, it's not "okay" for me to flip out
when somebody thinks they can get over on me
Oh, I beg to differ!
You can't expect us to be sweet
365 days of the year
especially when folks come with intentions
to make sweet girls shed tears in a world so cruel
that being sweet could mean being used
What are the sweet girls to do?
When acting sourly we get accused,
but it's okay for everyone else to break these rules
Well, the sweet girls are human too
and we're sick and tired of you fools
trying to chew us through
until we're ugly, bitter, and mean
Don't try to litter me
I will recycle your being
with the rest of the demons and thieves
who tried to commit burglary
by stealing all my sweet
but there is something
the sweet girls will never let you see
our own secret world
where we can be sweet
without having to worry
about this sour society
We will let you think we've changed
just so you can't bring any more pain

We will pretend you destroyed us,
mission complete
But then we'll take a voyage
to the forgiveness sea
I'm letting go for me
It doesn't mean that you can
take advantage of me
Trust me,
there is a time and place
when the sweet girls tuck their honey
and throw the sour in your face
so take it like you give it
and tell us how it tastes
That's what you get,
when a sweet girl's heart breaks.

Belong

Alicia Keys sang,
"A real man knows a real woman when he sees her."
Well then, these men must all be fake or blind
or let me guess I'm destined to
write one million heartbreak rhymes
as if forever always would make my ink run dry
Rather I live a lie than face my fright,
of spending alone all my days and nights?
But at the same time I don't want to fill a void
I said, I don't want a filler boy
My brother-figure says to focus on "I"
I try…
but my obsession with the term "mine"
to redefine I as we hypnotized my sights
until I could no longer see a me without a he
Without someone to belong to,
how can I, how can she be?
He replies, "Easily!"
Easily said, but not easily done my brother
It all began when I was very young, well… younger
This lover syndrome taking over me
In my eyes you may see one of the aspects of my life
that no girl should ever see, should ever feel
But I saw and I felt…
couldn't crawl into my shell, it was gone
Innocence down the wishing well
with all the other bronze
Searching for the love I no longer felt within myself
Yes, I was lost but… with a cause
because every single day since my will was jacked
been searching for a man to love me real, love me back
What do they call it? Oh, "the wrong track", I've been on it

Although as time passed, somehow I've finally re-grasped
the concept of loving me before loving he
and I do love me
but now I'm a grown woman
hungry for the concept of my own family
a home with a strong backbone
not broken like the only one I've known.

Slowly, Softly

Slowly, softly
undo the laces
of my corset
Show me I'm important
This "Open Mic" goes all night
Speak with your body,
be free from your mind
Slowly, softly
take your time
Don't push up on me
like those other guys
Don't pet name me "Mami",
call me your Wife
Don't climb upon me
just because you like
what you see between my thighs
Become one with me
because you like
what's inside my mind
Slowly, softly
massage my spine
Ease the pressure,
give me relaxation tonight
It isn't just about each inch
that goes inside
It's about the way you're doing it
while looking in my eyes
Believe me, I'll let you know it
when you're doing it right
Slowly, softly
is something you give to your bride
Turn off the cell phone,

the laptop, and the lights
Light the white candles
and the African Violet incense
set the aroma right
Massage oils on the bedpost
Baby, it's your flight…
number sixty-nine
After the foreplay,
this might be a bumpy ride
Take a window seat and watch me
slowly, softly
rock your crown
Honey, if you don't marry me
somebody else will
Slowly, softly
tell me you're for real
Show me what makes this different
from all of those cheap thrills
This ain't no six year stand
This ain't no booty-call,
and I'm not your groupie fan
Slowly, softly
kiss me everywhere you can
Yes, I want you in me
but first I need affection
I need expression
I need the connection
I need monogamy,
even when temptation tests it
I need a man who can come to church with me
not just come with me in the bed and
any man who deserves me will do anything

to bring me happiness
so if I catch you going too fast
you know that I'm not having it
Slowly, softly
put your back in it
Your right hand in my left hand,
tightly grabbing it,
strictly passionate
Don't let me catch you imagining
about any other woman
besides the one right here
This ain't no threesome,
all you need is right here
One queen equals every other woman
times infinity, keep your eyes right here
This isn't my insecurities,
this is me keeping it sincere
I know all about the conditioning
I know the dirty things the enemy
been whispering
That's why I need me a man who is
God-fearing
because I'm a God-fearing woman
and if you don't fear God
then why are you so scared
of love?
Slowly, softly
adjust my body
in the position that you want
Stop speaking English,
talk in the language of your heart
We can spend the whole weekend…

slowly, softly
letting down our guards
Let me be sure that I'm in love with
the man that you are
What have you been hiding from me?
I thought I was the pages in your diary
Somethings missing,
where is the part about us committing?
What are the reasons
why we keep coming
back to the bridge?
Going through phases of rekindling
instead of making plans for marrying,
futuristic baby carrying
when there is no comparison
to this love that grew
slowly, softly over the years
I'm still in love with you
but that doesn't mean
I'm going to shed
unconditional tears
while I wait to hear
the magic question
or at least have confirmation
that the time is near
Tomorrow isn't promised
just because we don't see
the expiration date
doesn't mean there isn't one on it
so think, before you hesitate
Can we, slowly softly
elevate to another level

when we're already past this
You love my physical vessel
but will you love me when old age hits?
Slowly, softly
tell me what it is, what's it going to be?
Are you my husband or
just another sin between the sheets
Slowly, softly
tell me you're in love with me,
what does it all mean?
Show me you're in love with me,
take initiative with action
to manifest our dreams
I don't want to wake up again
without you
slowly, softly
making love to me
Slowly, softly
rubbing me
going underneath the covers
drinking me like sweet nectar
Don't leave me lingering on fantasy
Trust me, the real thing is always better
I don't need to remember the last time
I need to feel it right here and now
I need you to be there, in my life now
Someway, somehow
you... I... we will make way
Slowly, softly
lead me across this bridge today
Let us pray along every step we take
into each unfamiliar place

Slowly, softly
reach to the other side
Don't fall off now, we've come too far
for looking behind
Just keep pushing forward
slowly, softly
just the way I like
Good things come
to those who try
Don't be scared to go deep
with me this time
Slowly, softly
kiss the tears from my eyes
Tell me king,
am I alone on this journey,
or are you by my side?
I'd rather you hurt me
than live the softest, sweetest lie
Please,
slowly, softly
bring the truth to light.

Senselessly Lovin' You

Oh, I wish I could come down to my senses
break it down to you in just one sentence
Got to quit pretending, quit extending
this invitation that I seem too busy to be accepting
It's no coincidence how I'm everywhere but there
and it may appear that I just don't care
but that's really not the truth
The problem here is that I'll still be loving you,
plus you'll still be loving me
So what makes you think
this time will flow differently?
Like we were ever really just a friend thing
I broke up with you years ago but we…
never really ended, did we?
Emotionally still tied to the way it used to be then
It's like an explosion when we link up
after you've been away from me,
all comes rushing back to me
Now, tell me what happens to gravity
every time you come around?
Acting like my man
then you leave back out of town
Baby, don't get me wrong…
I know you've got to rock them Mics,
but this here is my heart!
Don't you think it's time
to either put a ring on it or just let it go?
I'm done thinking about it
I kind of like being alone,
meditating on my life so I can get things right
Now here you come out the blue
surprising me with a visit, what am I to do?

Don't you see?
I'm living my life quite differently
since you've been gone
Don't you see? I'm practicing celibacy,
waiting for a man equally yoked in God?
Please tell me what do you want?
After all these years,
rekindling three dozen times
just to wind up right back here
Got me looking at this Pandora Box
saying hell to the no, keep that thing locked
Once it comes open, I know it won't stop
Chemistry flowing like it always did
then you want to know why I won't kiss your lips
so I've got to try to find the words to explain all of this
That isn't the type of predicament
I care to find myself dealing with
at this moment I'm on the chill
but how do I keep it real
without hurting someone I love so much?
I know the way you feel about me but...
I can't let that be my crutch
like you will always be there no matter what
No see, I've got to stand on my own two feet
waiting patiently for the man God has for me
as much as I'd like for him to be you
After all these years, I just can't believe that to be true
It takes more than just love...
without some kind of plan,
what's to ever come of us?
No one to blame
No pointing fingers

Clearly we've both had our faults
We've had our talks,
a couple of times we've even fought
but most of all, we've had real love
the kind I couldn't help but treasure
not to mention the intensity of our pleasure
But just because nobody has done me better
doesn't mean that this can be forever
How do I rationalize the reasons why
something so beautiful just has to die?
Feel like I'm clipping the wings off a butterfly
so it can no longer fly across the sky
In reality I'm just trying to find
a way to just look you in your eyes
while battling what I feel inside
and tell you I've made up my mind
Now, I know you didn't travel thousands of miles
just for me to tell you our love has gone out of style
Baby, you know we've worn that thing for a while
but I think it's time for us to change
This all could come with less pain
if you could just come down to your senses,
surely you'd feel the same
But we've both been senseless
It's so hard to break somebodies heart
in just one sentence
when you really care about them
but you know it's time to end it
and you're so scared
that you're about to lose your best friend.

IT

I used to think it was this woman ability
to be hurt repeatedly and still be able to find it in me
to give the next man a clean slate,
sanitized from the last man's dirt
but now I realize...
even Superwoman has her last nerve worked
Her last straw to the camel's back
Her last broken heart before the lifeline goes flat
but somehow the last time I died,
I came back to life more bubbly than before
yet my body was shut down
from anything that wasn't a spiritual force
So when you touch me there,
I don't think it is that I don't want it anymore
I just think that I need something more,
than the physical vessel is lusting for
Sometimes I feel invisible,
like you all can see my body but don't see my soul
I want something more than sex can offer me
even if the man who wants me
is a man who has never done anything wrong to me
Deep down, I still stand by God's beliefs
I think we should be married and take each other seriously
I'm tired of doing things against my humanity
but then we make excuses
like the conditioning is really the sanity
so we excuse ourselves from fornication
blame it on mother nature and see...
we're all just dying out here
If it isn't from some sexually transmitted disease,
it's from broken homes triggering violence on these streets,
pollution and poverty, and we think divorce is a normality

I feel like the right man should empower me
I feel like he should ask Daddy,
for my hand and make him proud of me
I think it is time for me to at least start thinking about…
really making plans to have a family
I just don't want to be that woman who gets so caught up
in everything business wise and material luxuries
that I forget about my maternal needs
My bio clock is ticking,
echoing like those leaky faucets in my heart been
I'm praying to God for guidance
when these chemical reactions have me ready to bargain
I'm getting tired of this long wind, Lord cut me some slack
See, I'm all wind burnt and I just need to relax
but every time I lay low, I feel so alone
like there is just too much space in this bed
and not enough testosterone
Most nights I'm focused on making love to microphones
but every time I go home after hours of being told,
I'm so talented and beautiful, and how the crowd loves me so
I realize that I'm still… rolling solo
because I won't settle for none of these rude boys
I'm so done trying to churn man out of boys
You know I have grown to be too much woman
to come between God and the men who continue to toy
with women who think they can change his ways
Look, I can plant seeds and drop jewels
but I can't thief-to-king a man who will never choose
It isn't my job to hold a gun to their heads, make sure they do
I've wasted too much energy
in my life thinking I could heal the same guys
who put me through the same things

my artistry had to pull me through
Now I finally know I'm beautiful
in every little way, shape, and form
even when I'm having a bad day, and show my thorns
I'm still the rose that fought these weeds to death
You could say I grew from the concrete, most definitely blessed
but there's a lot of things you can't see
Deep inside of all this skin,
 there is a spirit and until she is caressed
she wants nothing to do
with this meaningless sex and emptiness
If there is a man to get me pregnant,
he better be the man prepared for marriage
Not that, this would be the reason but...
I wouldn't be sleeping with a man
I wouldn't want to be with period
See, I don't need a brother who is unsure if he wants kids
because I'm positive, I do
I have learned the hard way,
I can't fly off buildings
to come to your rescue
but I have earned the rights to say
that I can build with you
I can be the woman to give you, all my love
but you've got to show me you're serious, in some other way
because eventually, my ring finger is going to get itchy
I don't want to settle for the second best, baby I need a king
If you haven't made up your mind just yet,
here are few things...
I love you. I need you. I would never leave you.
We're just ordinary people, reaching for the sequel
because we've been here so many times

and we'd be damn near blind
not to sit and wonder why
Maybe it really was meant to be you and I
Am I really just crazy, or are you the sanity in my life?
If you love me it just wouldn't be right,
spending my life by someone else's side
If you love me, show me the will
to make way to an eternity of paradise
Frankly, I'm so tired of being hurt and broken
by these other guys in between times
then you coming back to rescue me one last time
I guess the label "best friend",
is cutting off a whole lot of stuff
True, you were my right-hand man
when nobody else was
but you were my lover time and time again,
in between those other duds
They never lasted, but we always did
Now I'm just asking God, if this is really it?

Mr. Right Now

I used to say I wasn't looking for "Mr. Right Now"...
but now I think that is exactly what I need
Hold on a minute, before you jump the gun
and start letting the bullets of scrutiny fly at me
Please give me a chance to breathe
Usually I feel like people don't hear me clearly
no matter how sharp my point cuts across
I'm baring rugged heart in my poems
This is not to look hot or show off
how many words I can rhyme with metaphors
and how mine flows smoother than the chick before
But I realized tonight I had it all backwards
Thinking so far into the future that finding a man today,
to grow with tomorrow could be near impossible
See, the most recent guy only took two months
for cold feet to inspire this whole explanation
for how he's just not ready for me
How my presence is powerful and has him intrigued
How I'm one in a million but he's still leaving me
How he's lagging behind me and can't be with me this way
So I tried to tell him, the only moment promised was today
and that he should love for the now and that
I'm not saying to keep your head in the clouds
I'm just saying tomorrow is a treasure not yet found
so take the gold you have in your hands right now
because being "ready" is an illusion that constitutes failure
The genius of choice is in the choosing
not in waiting for perfection tailored
as if you are ever going to find a perfect fit
more perfect than God's gift of alignment
for two to become one
He forgot about our stronger connection

or maybe that was what scared him to begin with
A bond so fierce that he'd respond to my thoughts
with verbal replies
and sitting together felt like Tantra
like I have loved him in another life
and found him again
So I ask him how am I supposed to let this go?
Giving up something so special is like subjecting self to the trap
perceiving time as this thing we'll always have
as we know it here
Time is like a mat that could get pulled any day of the year
I'm not saying to give up the fears
but facing them is now or never
See, when I say I want Mr. Right Now, it means I know better
Yes, I wanted each kiss to be eternal
Yes, I admit there were hopes that someday we'd get married,
have kids and achieve all our dreams but seriously…
what girl-to-woman doesn't have these?
What person doesn't long to see those days?
I just needed you to live for today, plan for the next
Don't make the assumption that you're immune from death
If you understand then why are you sleeping on love
like you haven't found it yet?
With everything I've been through and stood strong,
surely there's a man who can stand with me
Surely Mr. Right Now will not wimp out,
of this moment that may never come again
If it does in the morning, then each breath should be like new
See, Mr. Right Now isn't a one night stand
but rather the beginning to the end of being hurt again
because a man who lives for right now
won't take me for granted

like the man who thinks he can do damage
that can be fixed some other day
Mr. Right Now won't sacrifice our present chances,
for moments never traced
Right now, I just wish I knew where you were
I wish you would stop living for man's clock,
and start ticking with the earth.

Because Hip Hop Broke My Heart

He asked me what I missed when I thought of him
I responded, "All of the things, we never did,
the moments we never shared, like marriage
and the things we also did...
like French toast, in the morning time
like shopping for clothes, both looking fly
sharing our dreams of rocking Mics
reminiscing on how Hip Hop was our original ties."
But baby, Hip Hop couldn't tie the knot
when the record stopped spinning
and my heart wouldn't defrost
And Hip Hop didn't go to church with me
when I got saved
Hip Hop didn't know how much he hurt me
when I felt alone on all his tour dates
Hip Hop went commercial on me
when I didn't want to just make a "hit"
but wanted to bring things back to real music
Hip Hop didn't understand
how badly I wished we could have had kids
if he was home enough to be a daddy
in between the remix
This is the real life *Brown Sugar*,
the parts that got cut out
This isn't a movie dramatized,
I'll tell you what it's all about
This is a woman tired of
"Always being your boo"
sitting here missing that old school
when rhyming had substance
the way that lovers used to....
Even R&B just wants me to grind with you

So what's the lyrics of my life to do?
How do they live on when our Hip Hop died?
When Isley Brother's sing the tears from my eyes
and I'm wishing "Make Me Say It Again Girl",
would be the words in your mind
pressed against your lips the way I always was
and Silk reminds me of us with "Let's Make Love"
So you want to hear me "tell you that it's all mine"...
but unfortunately, the lack of 112's "Let's Get Married"
has me taking flight
I thought I already told y'all the first time
when I wrote "Broken Records"
But it seems like my heavy emotions
drift, light like feathers
and you don't even catch them
when they fall
See, Hip Hop is in recession,
and you've just been laid off
But like Tupac feat. Jon B you ask me,
"Are You Still Down?"
Then you pull a Silk move,
"Let me Lick you Up And Down"
You miss "LSG'ing" My Body
But Hip Hop never got the crown
I went Poetry on y'all,
so you can call me soft
but I guarantee to reach the people
with more than sixteen bars
You light me like
Sixteen Candles in my heart
burning with fire, feeling the rage
Covered in the blood of Jesus

from a bucket filled with pain
then Hip Hop has the nerve
to spray paint the walls I just cleaned off today
Just to leave me "tagged"
So then I have to put in over time
Pull out the "Le'Andria Johnson" track
Begin to testify, "JESUS!"
Getting down on my knees
Begging the Lord to please forgive me
for tramp stamping my poetry
with his name inked on the spine
of these words I write
See Hip Hop did permanent damage
to my skin
Keep scrubbing it off,
but it just rubs in
So tell me Hip Hop,
from which deck of cards are we playing?
Because it seems like we're living
in a full house of Satan
but Kim Burrell keeps me saying,
"yes to his will"
when Hip Hop tries to deceive me
like when Tupac and Biggie got killed
and Jaheim chills my soul
like a hot Chai tea latte
when the nights get cold
singing "Ready, willing, and able"
taking the rhythm nice and slow
then his joint, feat Mary J.
"Beauty and a THUG",
makes me remember how people can change

Even if Hip Hop looks like a beast,
the right lips might kiss away this phase
but then Hip Hop keeps
coming with the same old game
Asking me why things can't be "the same"
because it should have never been this way
What happened to the passion?
Were we doing more than rapping?
Were we emcees, or just as guilty
as these new school newbies?
Where did the buzz of our love come from?
From Brooklyn to Connecticut
had me driving to the hood just to represent
Six years of being your open book to express
Thirteen years of writing dope lyrics
Hip Hop looked good but couldn't cut a check
We always kept it hood during each "duet"
but maybe Hip Hop should, just speak to my neck
if he isn't ready yet, like Keith Sweat
Baby, there is a right
and a wrong way to love
And while it's true, I might be young
I'm the roots of real Hip Hop
"Not a little girl, I'm a woman"
But you aren't grown yet?
Maybe Hip Hop, needs to step off stage
Do some soul-searching
break dance away when
"It's Gonna Rain"

Kelly Price set the records straight
There is something that Hip Hop must know
so listen to me while I spit this scroll
See… without God as the center of our love,
our Hip Hop is in vain
so if you never plan on being saved
then baby, Hip Hop better off
bobbing his head to cats with
their platinum chains
When did the gold temple within
get played out for this level of sin?
When did Hip Hop forget our stories
were supposed to give God the glory
and help us find the way,
out of our ghetto pasts?
See Hip Hop,
you aren't about to be my "Baby Dad"
If Hip Hop can't give his last name
to symbolize what we have
then Hip Hop, all I have to say
is I'm tired of this track
and would rather get me some
Brownstone "If You Love Me",
than sign some wack contract
So just cut your percent,
and blame Hip Hop
for the moments we never had
But I thank God my poetry roots grew back
and are forever steadfast
As a matter of fact,
take your Hip Hop pen back.

Moving On

He was the one, made me break
always be your boo promises
once made in another headspace,
time, place, before this love took its place
Clearly, we were just water paint…
carried away, thinking we had that stuff
Had me hung-up,
amused by our colorful mess,
dripping wet…
never seeming to dry quite right,
but we tried.
Not to say you were just some guy,
but that thing they say about hindsight
sure rings true
when I think of you
I think of me
being so naïve,
doing things for your pleasure
that chipped away at me, secretly
Knowing what we were there for
Selling myself short…
I knew one day,
I would not love you anymore
Reshuffling the same deck of cards
We had played out
every possible version of us
but he was the one who won my heart
when our game wasn't working
Countless losses
when we were never in it to win
to begin with
We stayed for the moment,

for the thrill,
for the fill
like a one-night stand on repeat
for those years
Not to say we didn't shed tears
when goodbye was the only thing
left to say
but you being my boo
was getting in the way
of finding something more
I remember
when I closed that door
not knowing
when the right one would open
Lonely and heartbroken
until he came and split our soul ties open
Loosening the knots on false forever's
You don't want to hear it,
but I've found something better
Call him my one and only,
spending life together
What did you expect?
Some promises
weren't made
to be kept.

Sweet Irony

Well, I'm sorry if it makes you uncomfortable
when I'm baring my heart and soul
Go ahead, call me so emotional
out of control, but you don't know…
what it's like to be a woman in this day and age
when the world has the values of love misplaced
Now baby,
please don't hurt me, leave me, or desert me
I just think our anniversary would be a good time
to get it together if you know what I mean
You see the look in my eyes,
trying to weather a storm of passionate beliefs
So maybe it's between God and me
because I can't make you see
or make you be ready
but maybe there are some decisions to be made
Should I hold out on this here until our wedding day?
Go back to celibacy despite the situation
Lord, it drives me crazy
how he can rock with me like this
but isn't quite ready for that Holy matrimony kiss
although he says it will be soon
I'm so anxious to say, "I do!"
and I don't want to continue living in sin
although it's hard when your heart
already considers that man your husband
but according to God we haven't tied the knot
until we take those vows before Him
Got my man telling me to put a little trust in him
wondering why I'm so worried
when I know I've got the one in him
but it's a spiritual war when you want to please the Lord

Plus, you don't want to be the girlfriend anymore
when I've spiritually matured far beyond that position
Trying to find the right words to tell you what we're missing
You'll have to see for yourself
I won't bring this up again as time will tell
if this love will transcend beyond worldly limitations
but I won't sit around waiting
After all… you should be the one still chasing after me
thinking, "Will she say yes?" when you get on one knee
but I guess we'll see…
because by then, I might need time to think
Well, wouldn't that be sweet irony?

Poetess in Love

The rupturing heart of a poetess
is not to be possessed by those
with a weakness of pride
Her words may be piercing
like the sun in the morning time
invading your space
although it means you no harm
In fact, without it there would be nothing
but in the moment when you'd rather
pull the covers over your head
to migrate back to dreamland
than submit to the torturous beauty of sunlight,
that truth matters not
And in the moment,
when her emotions seem to gush like
waterfalls from foreign mountains
in languages that are as disturbingly exotic
as they are intriguing
it can be difficult to process, I understand
It's fine when she puts it in a poem
It's safe there, shielded by the code of art
where freedom of expression is her prerogative
but when those feelings leave the poem
and penetrate conversation...
it's not just a poem anymore,
now it's personal
and you are expected to respond
because she is more than just a poetess
She is...
human, lover, helper, wife, mother
She is a poetess, in love with you.

The Expressionist

She sits across a table from him
trying to master the art
of batting tears back into her eyes
One escapes…
hits heavy on her leg
like tiny rocks from tall buildings
The expressionist fails again.
It's so frustrating…
delivering honesty
to someone who'd rather,
"bees with honey" or plain lies
Though she didn't catch any bees,
she also didn't sell any soul
but the bittersweet silence rips her open
Emotions begin to swarm the thoughts
that urge her to articulate
the words to express
the many layers of feelings within
She's barely scraped the surface
when he appears to be drowning,
so how can she go deeper?
Now the both of them are suffocating
when his too much is her not enough
He's overwhelmed
She's incomplete
knowing that she is not being
received
At least,
not in the way she intended to be
and that look on his face…
she hates that look
like he sees her differently

like he was having an epiphany
She wished he would…
then maybe he'd get it!
But you can't bring a message
to someone not ready to accept it
Raise an issue with them...
they'll act like you've
got the wrong address
and they won't address it
Maybe some other time, she thinks
as she digs through her purse
for lip-gloss,
searching for solace
It works for a moment…
but in her heart there is nothing
to conceal the pain
and though she holds herself
together quite well,
the expressionist feels everything
"Don't take it to heart," he says
She looks up at him,
says nothing…
but her expression says it all.

The Edge

She's at the edge…
adrenaline rushing, eyes sparkling
as moonlit streams of tears keep flowing
She has lost all hope
in that which kept her going
so why you ask, is she praying
to the "All-Knowing"?
Because, while her hope is broken,
she still has her faith
although she doesn't know if
she can take another day living… this way
being hurt by the one who says, "I love you."
But it's like… she is spirit, he is flesh
in a constant warfare against each other
Soul sister in love, with a carnal brother
So stuck in his skin that he can't see,
the way his actions go against her whole design
and he receives her having passion
as a threat to his ego
so his defenses go up the instant she tries
to speak wisdom on an issue but he doesn't have time
That's why he slams doors on her open heart
and sees it as his right as her emotions pour
then the battle starts
The two of them can't talk
They don't even get along
but the connection that binds them is strong
so walking out on this love is not a painless task
but she's ready to give it all up
if he keeps putting her heart out like the trash
Where is her value in a home of misplaced aggression?
All the times he disrespected or left her neglected

All the words said, things done
No acceptance of hurting the woman he loves
The wounds run so deep within,
that you'll never see them on her skin
so it's easy for him to pretend
from the outside looking in
that he's done nothing
But she's at the edge...
ready to give up on him
desert him physically
the way he has deserted her emotionally
Only then will he understand
Only then will she have drawn
the line in the sand
He doesn't even know it
but she's leaving him…
on the edge
where she has been time and time again
Only then will he understand
what it's like to be on her end
Only then will he be defeated,
and only then will they begin again.

Gone Dry

Red eyes, ashy lips
from crying all night
while you're on the dream lift
Looking all peace while I'm torn in pieces
Tell me this love hasn't *gone dry*
Tell me there's a refill on this kind
Drinking water done no justice
Its skin, soul, and passion I need
There's no sign of you quenching me
We cross paths silently
like enemies just keeping peace
just as long as nobody's crossing territory
coming too close for comfort
There's a current I keep going under
Waving, flailing arms around
hoping you might save me now
If you love me, would you let me drown
or has your heart *gone dry*?
Used to be so wet with excitement
to see me after your shift ends
Lord, tell me this isn't the end
I'm not one for just going through motions
void of the defining emotion
nor do I want to do it for the kids
Tell me you'd still be here
if it weren't for our children
because I can't bear to be up in this place
being treated like I'm a big disgrace
when I'm the reason
we've made it this far in the first place
because you came into this
with one foot out the door

Afraid to lose yourself,
always ready to move forward
while I have completely committed
Not to mention how I've handled our business...
total management of yours and mine,
making sure everything is paid on time
and you act like I don't be cooking and cleaning
making love every evening
up until you decided to get high on yourself
like you're fine all by yourself
Lie to yourself like you've *gone dry*
No desire for the good love we used to share
I wonder, the last fight... did I lose you there?
Or did our flame die, wax *gone dry*
just playing house like we cared?
Is this the sole cause or just the last straw?
Either way I'm not leaving even if you are
My heart's staying here
I didn't put in all these years,
sacrifice so much for the sake of us
just to walk away like it don't mean nothing
Don't it mean something?
Or has the original essence of our love *gone dry*
Well, if that's the case may we be redefined
You ask me who I'm talking to
Shoot, I'm in my *"War Room"*...
praying, asking the Lord to fight my battles for me
When everything *gone dry*, he will reign
Let it rain down on you and I
May the soils of this love be fruitful and rich
May only the right seeds be planted
Help us stop taking our marriage for granted

Let him see where he's gone wrong
Show him home is in my arms
and that without me in his life, he would be so gone
I'm not going out with a broken heart, not like this
While reconciliation takes two
there's nothing a God as great as mine can't do
So I'll be still and let Him move
My faith hasn't *gone dry*
despite tests we've been through
See, I can quit jobs and bad habits
but I can't quit you
No matter how dry this thing gone
the will to thrive lies in our roots
making way for higher ground
Don't love me when I'm gone,
love me right now
You talking all that talk,
while I'm talking about vows
Why let a love be lost,
that was made to be found?

War Room

I knew a man…
said he wanted peace
but was always bringing war
Spitting fire
and he called it "tough love"
But baby,
It burned just the same

She could prophesize
in the language
of his own heart
and he still wouldn't understand
Not if it meant he had to change
Lie down the double-edged sword
Give up the game
Turn himself over to the Lord

Even when she told him
she doesn't want to be hurt no more
He couldn't bear the thought
of power lost
Tripping on control,
that's all he really wants

He'll do anything to get it
No remorse, he don't regret it
He'll hold his sin over your head,
if you let him

But I told that man…

I'm not responsible
for the mass destruction
I told him,
"You can go if you want to go."
But God knows I love him

Leaving him was never an option
I only kept that a secret
to protect what was left
I prayed every prayer
a good woman could pray
This is spiritual warfare,
there ain't no time to play

Satan got a hold on my man
Ladies, do you understand?
When he speaks to me like that
I feel the demons on his breath
then he says he wants peace
while attacking me to death

so I know
this here requires
me to stand my position
Put on my armor
Satan can't win him

He's my man
and I will stand in his corner
until this war is over

He may think I'm coming at him
when I'm defending our love

I've been so tired of him snapping
Always mad at me, I've had enough
Walking on thin ice
Scared to talk to my own man

But now I see it's all the Devil
trying to win his hand
Hell, no! You'd better go!
Because the only blood to be shed
is the blood of Jesus,
covering our marriage

Despite my disappointments
in what has been going on
I'll put up a fight for him
Lord, I know he's wrong
but I'm holding on to you
and letting go of me

My skin isn't thick enough
but my faith runs deep
So here I am...
looking just like me
Loaded,
with the Holy Spirit
Ready, to free the man I chose to love
from the enemy!

Love Prevails

Love…
Please have a seat beside me
Egos and pride aside, just trust in me
There is no battlefield between us
This spiritual warfare, we fight as one
Despite the issues set to divide us
I need you to realize…
I gave you my life, love
I stood by your side, love
I looked in your eyes, love
and we made vows promised
before the Most High, love
It was deeper than men in tuxes
and I dressed in all white, love
More complex than the celebration
with family and friends,
of the groom and the bride, love
And as beautiful as it all was…
It wasn't about the cake, or the gifts
It was us, choosing to love
beyond just a human emotion
A decision to never give up
no matter what,
we'd never lose our devotion
See baby…
I come from a home that was broken
I know the damage it does
to everyone involved
when people walkout on a love
for which they swore,
they would always hold down
I've witnessed betrayal in its worst forms

I've experienced the ways lust
can leave whole families torn
I've watched people walkout on their love
like it was nothing more
than a signed piece of paper that at any time,
could be replaced, by a case of divorce
Walking in self-righteousness,
dismissing the Lord
Not recognizing that not all worldly laws
are legitimate, according to His word
What's approved in a lawyer's office
doesn't necessarily register with God
in the spiritual realm
See, we would still be sinners
considered married
despite the lies they sell
Still soul-tied as husband and wife
even if we were with someone else
Even in situations of separation,
God's word commands us to stay alone
until we can come together again
Divorce is a man-made thing
People often forget about the pain it will bring
Too fixated on immediate gratification
to see the biggest mistake
of their lives in the making
Then one day they sit and say
"It didn't have to be this way."
It doesn't have to be this way,
we can pray our way through this
My heart can't stand another break
Like Sade, "Somebody already..."

You just don't know
what I've been through in my past
My soul was once lost on dark paths
on which I cannot turn back
I didn't go through the healing
or the deliverance
to be a broken spirit, all over again
I need you to love me right
without the spite, or the blame chip
Come gently to your wife,
baby, I can't take it
All this fire we've been playing with
like we're not each other's one and only
Like we didn't unite in holy matrimony
See those vows were not a game
and even as the seasons change...
our love must be unmovable,
always standing the rain
Nobody ever made it by just walking away
No matter how many reasons
there were to say goodbye
There was the voice of God saying "Try!"
and that, is the truth about why
some marriages die while others survive
With God as the center
His way, His will, will always provide
What it takes for love to prevail
against every odd in this life.

Forgiveness

Remedies for wounded spirits
don't always come on tongue tips
Verbal apologies are not the cure-all
for those moments
when you said what you said
Didn't mean it, but it slipped
You did what you did, wished you didn't…
but you've got to face the consequences
Claim the damages
Enter repentance, seek the mastermind to fix
what your humanity is powerless to fully mend
When your beloved holds a grudge,
the road seems to never end
but it's more than just the promise
that you'll never take it there again
It's the internalized sincerity that must exist
For your word is only as genuine
as the proceeding actions
so cry a river to your woman if you will
but you'd better give her the realness
or in due time the milk will spill
and reveal behind the mask,
the truth lives still
Seek the source to pull your cards,
dig out your heart of hearts
Cleanse the wicked from your thoughts
and bring forth a purer being
than the person you'll keep being
if you maintain a flesh-led life
Everything you love will be sacrificed
by the repetition
Please understand…

whether or not you'll be forgiven
is not a one-sided street
Bondage like this can run deep
and relationships can't survive on
another superficial "I'm sorry."

God's Hands

My dear,
we've both said things we didn't mean
but to live without this love
is to breathe without trees
Please don't let this world cut down the beauty
between you and me
You know I'm only a woman,
not perfect by any means
Some say, "Treat me like a Queen!"
but I say love me like Christ loved the church…
now that's "King"!
In relationships of my past I've been hurt
but baggage, I never meant to bring
so I'm retiring from that "Bag Lady" position
I've got a new one, seeking the Lord
on behalf of this commitment
I'm asking for and offering forgiveness
because we've both been wrong
in different ways
Acting like we want to be gone when
we wanted to stay
I know all couples have
their good days and bad days
but for the most part, it's been good
These words from my heart
shall not be misunderstood
Every relationship has rocky times
but can't nobody love me
like this man of mine
we've got history upon which
we can testify…

You know the loss of a baby
hasn't been easy on us
Sometimes it feels like…
I'm losing my mind
The pain runs so deep
but you've been right there by my side
no matter how hard it gets
But babe, I'm sorry for the times I've been less
than the woman God has called me to be
There have been moments I was blind
but now I see that you really do love me
so please don't give up on me, baby I have a plan…
let's turn this love over to God's hands.

Love in Real Time

I never realized how thin
the bitter layer of my heart was
until it came time for forgiving him
Thought I'd die in this prison within…
hanging on to times he said what???
Times when we was…
immature in love, insecure in love,
"A Dream Deferred" of love
Expectations surfaced…
pretty paintings peeled,
revealed we wasn't perfect
See, relationships can't survive
on first weekend vibes
Love takes a daily nurturer
tending to its elements to thrive
Lovers must give up on searching
for the first flicker of a love first born
and just… grow with love
Don't let go of love
"Wait… hold up,
where you going, Luv?"
Nothing I've ever known
comes close to us
I want this love in real time bad enough
to put what matters over mind
and release my grudge
If love keeps no record,
I'm giving mine up
Yes, your apologies accepted…
now it's time for making up
No sense in breaking up
to pretend this wasn't all it was

Rather spend energies praying for us
than bother arguing over things
discussed more than once
Bringing up years of mess-ups
like we're still stuck on issues
already worked through
So if I'm sorry I hurt you,
and you're sorry you hurt me
all that's left to do is live by what we speak
through how we treat one another,
even when we're angry
Got to make the one you love
feel special always
by any means necessary
even if it means
applying ancient wisdom,
while living in
a modern age love story.

ABOUT THE AUTHOR

Born in Connecticut, Tabitha Marie Long, better known on stage as Ms. Tabu, is a well-rounded writer and performance poet, writing her first poem at the young age of ten. She then discovered a new gift for rhythm and lyricism at thirteen and has been songwriting ever since. Not to mention her theatrical roots that stem from early childhood and have grown around her wordplay and envelop her artistic demeanor on stage.

For the audience, witnessing the real life inspired acts of Ms. Tabu can be like watching a clip from a dramatically enchanting play. In some of her writings, she focuses on interracial issues with pieces such as "I'm Not Worth Your Stereotypes," as she passionately promotes diversity through her nicely seasoned delivery of words. Both in and out of her artistry, Ms. Tabu is a humanitarian who advocates for social justice and equal rights. From her viewpoint, it is through her honesty and courageousness that others can be reached.

Extremely versatile, she also writes of many other subjects, such as ones pertaining to love, spirituality, and family. She takes lovers of her craft into her world to share her heart with them. Her work echoes of a soul being delivered from personal struggles, as she heals through each page of her life. She is both hip-hop and soulful with a touch of a woman's manifesto and a Free Verse style that lets her navigate from poetry to prose, making her a phenomenal performer.

Ms. Tabu has been featured at countless events and venues, mainly between Connecticut and New York City. On September 23rd 2010, Ms. Tabu successfully presented the grand debut of her show, "MIC2SOUL," which showcased new artists on a monthly basis.

A woman of many goals, Ms. Tabu is currently in the process of writing new content for *A Voyage to Love,* what will be the third book of the "Love Passages" series. She also has plans to record several Spoken Word albums based on the material in her books.

It would be easy for someone to assume that a person so artistically equipped would lack humility, but Ms. Tabu humbly perceives herself as a vessel with a purpose to deliver messages through her craft. She is on a God-given mission not only to give voice to the voiceless, but to instill healing and growth in people through relating experiences.

THANK YOU

Thank you for reading *Hot Pink Nail Polish and a Broken Heart*, the first book of the Love Passages series! Because reviews are critical in spreading the word about books, please leave a brief review expressing what you enjoyed most about it on Amazon, Barnes & Noble, or Goodreads.

For my eBook lovers, Kindle and Nook editions are also available.

If you haven't yet read the first book of the series, *Inkwells of Love,* get it now on Amazon or Barnes & Noble.

Stay tuned for the release of the third book of this ongoing series, *A Voyage to Love.*

Also by *Author* Ms. Tabu:
CROSS POINTS:
The Poetic Diary of Ms. Tabu

CONNECT

Want to know when I release new books and have book signings or special appearances? Here are some ways to stay updated:

Like me on Facebook:
www.facebook.com/MsTabu

Visit my website:
www.MsTabu.com

Follow me on Twitter:
@OfficialMsTabu

Follow me on Instagram:
@MsTabuOfficial

www.ingramcontent.com/pod-product-compliance
Lightning Source LLC
Chambersburg PA
CBHW051827040426
42447CB00006B/409